NAKED
AND
Unashamed

LEARNING
TO LIVE A
LIFE
UNCOVERED

KIMBERLY OLIVER

Charleston, SC
www.PalmettoPublishing.com

Memoir
Published and Printed in the United States of America
First edition

Paperback ISBN: 978-1-68515-754-8
eBook ISBN: 978-1-68515-755-5

Kimberly Oliver
Email: kimberly@livingfromtheheart.tv
Website: livingfromtheheart.tv

*All events described in this work are shared authentically
through the perceptions of the author. Some characters in
her story are not identified by their actual names.*

Acknowledgments

S O MANY PEOPLE HAVE CHEERED ME ON DURING THE SEASON OF writing this book, my story. I am blessed to be surrounded by such amazing, authentic people. It is truly a gift from above. I have fallen in love with my life again and have shown up brave. Thank you, wonderful friends, who have been cheerleaders throughout my life. I also am grateful for the pain I walked through because it has helped me become the person I am today.

I am grateful for....

- My Lord and Savior Jesus Christ – You always forgive me and show me who I am in You.

- My mom – You were always my cheerleader.

- My two boys, Sean and Jered Harlan, who have given me a *why* my entire life. You boys are the reason I have never quit. You have been my inspiration as we have walked through life and its seasons. Thank you for always believing in me, even though I have blown it a million times. Thank you for turning out so amazing despite my shortcomings as your mother. I am grateful that your love for me has always been greater than my imperfections. I was not a perfect mom, but my love for you was perfect.

*My grandson Brock! Brock, you gave me a reason to keep going and never give up because of your innocence. You are a rock star to Kiki, and I am forever grateful for you! I love you deeply.

*Bob Hamp, my therapist, who helped me find *me* again after going through the darkest season of my adult life. Thank you for helping me see things differently. Thank you for helping me see life from a different perspective.

*My Keller Williams family for being family to me when I felt I had no one. You always showed up for me.

*Carol Anderson Ward for giving me a safe place when I desperately needed it. Thank you for sharing your beautiful horses with me and Brock. You inspired me as a woman and gave me hope in the darkest season of my life. Much healing came on Fletcher Road. Thank you for being there for me.

*Miquette Martinez, owner of my Keller Williams office, for always being *my person*. In the most difficult times, you cheered me on and reminded me of my worth. You always saw the gifts in me that I couldn't see or feel. Thank you!

*To my many friends whom I call my tribe. Each one of you have given me room and met my need to belong. You are my people, the people I do life with. Thank you all!

*Brené Brown for the amazing books, Ted Talks, and research you have done on vulnerability. It is through you I have learned to own my brokenness, show up, and be brave. I champion you and your work. You do make a difference! I would love to meet you someday.

ℯ   My Book Project Team: Justin and Paige Collins for the amazing book launch video and photography you captured. Shannon Butler of Sundance Concepts for your creative edge on the book cover design. I am grateful for you.

ℯ   My adversaries…. Thank you for the pain and abandonment you left me to feel. The power I once gave you over me has since compelled me to learn how to be myself again. There are a lifetime of painful encounters. I have learned from each of them—and that's how I can be grateful for the pain. I see you as a blessing now because you pushed me to become me.

Foreword

I N THE EARLY DAYS OF CHRISTIANITY, NO ONE STOOD ON STAGES or broadcast from screens. Normal people lived their normal lives and shared deeply of the stories that moved them from normal to beloved. It was one man or one woman telling their ordinary stories that spread the extraordinary love of God across the entire planet.

Kimberly Oliver has done both. She has stood on platforms, but she has also lived the life we all lead. Sometimes painful and confusing, but also filled with joy and love, these experiences weave together to create the kind of life that tells the story of being human in a fallen world and a redeemed Kingdom. Kimberly tells her story in a way that helps us see that life is neither good nor bad; it is simply life. From the confusion of early sexual abuse and the ways the abuse shaped her picture of herself, through the adult years of finding healing and finding (and losing) love, Kimberly helps us see the Jesus who is "God-With-Us" in every possible experience of life.

Kimberly is honest and holds nothing back. Her story moves from hope to pain to redemption and shows the constancy and growth of a life lived in Christ. This is no "broken to healed" story. Kimberly's story is much more the broken AND healed story of us all.

With no fear and no shame, Kimberly lets us in behind the curtain to see the reverse of what happened to Adam and Eve in the garden. Her story moves us from "eyes opened and ashamed" to Naked and Unashamed.

Bob Hamp, MMFT, LMFT
Think Differently Counseling, Consulting, and
Connecting Center
Grapevine, Texas

A note to the reader from my heart ...

I AM A NORMAL PERSON JUST LIKE you. I have gone through life with pain, rejection, abandonment, abuse, heartbreak, and self-destruction. Writing this book about my personal journey has been on my heart for the last 15 years. My plans were interrupted many times, and I put my dream on a shelf, haunted by feelings that I was unworthy and unqualified to even tell my story. The nudge always returned, and over the years has convinced me that I am in fact supposed to complete this book—and finally, here I am. I am not sure what happens from here, but I know if I can help just one person, it was all worth it.

When I learn of someone who has been through heartache and pain, I empathize. Then their pain inspires me to do more, to be more, and to persevere more. Many of us don't want to share our struggle. After all, struggle isn't pretty. Struggle isn't wrapped in bliss. Struggle is often sad, lonely, or messy. But, when we hear how achievement has come alongside struggle, hope is born. In contrast, when we attach shame to our struggle, we tend to wear our story as our identity, rather than what it REALLY is…. just an experience that is simply a part of our story.

When we choose to make something better of our story, we find inner strength. Then we become a source of inspiration for others who are walking through life believing that their mess could never be cleaned up and God couldn't save them from the destruction they have caused. He can and He will because he LOVES you. He knows you. Our hustle then becomes to learn, grow, and win ourselves back. We must fight to find our authentic self and fall in love with who we are, no matter where we come from. We are all on a journey, and no one can truthfully say, "I have the perfect life, and everything is perfect." That's just the makings of Hallmark movies.

We all have a desire to belong, to be heard, to be loved unconditionally, and have the life we dream of. I found I could fulfill my dreams, but I had to fight for them! Our poor attitudes, false beliefs, unrealistic expectations, and our negative mindsets so often hold us back. We may tell ourselves stories birthed during a time of disappointment or heartbreak. Yes, events in life will hurt. But we must ask ourselves, *what did I learn? How did I grow from it?* We are not helpless; rather, we can create the life of our dreams.

I must give a huge shout out to Joyce Meyer, an amazing author, minister, and mentor to many through her TV programs and other media broadcasts. I have never met her, however 25 years ago, the trajectory of my life shifted when I began following her and listening to her teachings. I heard her story, and it inspired me. She shared the darkest moments of her life and in her willingness to show up brave, she saved my life. She changed my life, just as she has for countless other woman. I remember thinking, *if God did it for her, he will do it for me.* Her story gave me hope and courage. I didn't feel isolated anymore. The more I spoke to women around me, I learned they had stories too. We all do.

One in four women have a story like mine. I am no more special than the next girl. Who I am is a girl with a story who dared to put it out there, understanding that showing up to fight for myself will bring criticism. But I can embrace that as well. I am inspired by authors and researchers like Brené Brown. I love her work and research on vulnerability and courage. Being brave requires being vulnerable. Being vulnerable means you may get your ass kicked and your heart might get broken.

I have learned that if we keep seeking first to understand, we mature and grow. We were never promised an easy life. We were promised that if we will have faith, even as small as a mustard seed, all things will work together for our good. As you read my story, it is my prayer that you find your own authenticity. It does not matter what you have gone through or what you have done; what matters is that you keep seeking to understand and that you don't stop growing. This principle carried me through my journey.

My goal in revealing my raw, authentic story through *Naked and Unashamed* is to inspire you to JUST DO YOU. No one has a story exactly like yours. You are uniquely made, and you are valued. Be yourself. I say… YOU DO YOU, BOO.

Kimberly Perdue Oliver

Contents

Chapter One

INNOCENCE STOLEN

I WAS NOT RAISED IN CHURCH. I DID NOT HAVE THE FAMILY STRUC-ture that many had. But I craved it—deeply. My mom always said I was the entertainer, even as a little girl. I think I arrived on the scene believing I had a destiny of importance, not out of arrogance, just a desire to GO BIG in whatever my heart was set on in the moment.

I dreamed of being on TV and fantasized about being the lead actress in major movies. Even as a child, I recognized my passion to entertain people. An innate people-person, entertaining others was a natural way to connect. When I played with my dolls, I would act out my dreams with them, pretending we were a family. First, it was my Thumbelina doll who I carried around everywhere, and then it was Barbie. I had every style of Barbie that came out, and I loved dressing them in the latest Barbie fashions. I just knew that when I grew up my Ken would be equally as handsome as hers, and the world would be wide open to us. My imagination never lacked the element of dreaming big.

I came into this world June 28, 1964 in Dallas, Texas. I grew up in Grand Prairie, a suburb of Dallas, which made our small town seem tiny compared to the big city. Mom said I was a very good baby. The oldest child, I got to be the only child for five years. I learned to play alone well, which only fostered my huge imagination. As a child I always felt there was something greater than myself. I had an adventurous soul. I loved to make people laugh, to sing, and to perform for my family. I thought I could sing quite well. The truth is I am tone deaf, but I never knew. In my innocence, I saw myself as a rising star. So, I used any toy I could find as a microphone.

I still remember putting on shows for my mom and grandparents. My grandfather, JW Parker (Paw-Paw), used to grin at me as only he could. I felt the warmth of his adoration, even though he never said anything. My grandfather was a man of few words. He was not overly affectionate, but I knew he loved me just by the way he looked at me and smiled. I am the only grandchild he never spanked, which has become a running joke in our family. I felt his favor back then, and it stayed with me into adulthood. Being the first grandchild, I was loved and adored.

My grandparents got to practice on me, and they were young grandparents when I came along. I spent a lot of time with my them as my mom was young when I came into the world. My grandmother, Ellen Oliver Parker, was my hero and the rock of my life. I called her Mimi. She passed away in February 2014, and I miss her dearly. I pray I can carry on the role of grandmother to my grandchildren the way she modeled it to me.

My toddler years were vivid. There were times I had a wonderful life, and there were times when my childhood was like an awful movie—dark and chaotic. My first memory is from approximately age three. I experienced things an innocent toddler should not experience. I will tell you about that later.

I grew up with a very girlie side, and I owe that to my Mimi. I played dress up in her closet every time I went to her home. She had every color of pump I could imagine. When going to her and PawPaw's home, I would think of the outfits I could put together. It was always an adventure going to Mimi's, and I always looked forward to seeing them. Pawpaw and Mimi's house was my safe place. She allowed me to wear her pearls, and I would sneak on her wedding rings and pretend I was rich because I perceived my grandparents to be wealthy people. In truth, they were middle class Americans. But in my eyes, they were every-thing. Her wedding ring looked so huge to me back then. I know now, it was less than a half carat. But I presumed it to be the largest diamond in the world. I loved playing the role of a grown up. Every time I went to Mimi's house, I drug out her high-heel shoes and walked around feeling all grown up. She was quite the fashion queen in my eyes.

PawPaw, however, was very stern and serious most of the time. He was a police officer in the city. He was one of the first motorcycle officers in Grand Prairie. I remember listening to him chase the bad guys on the police radio. I thought my PawPaw was famous. My Mimi worked at the courthouse, and she seemed to be an important person as well. She worked for the Justice of the Peace, and her large office was next to a judge's. I visited her and saw the judge draped in his robe. I had seen people in a court room on TV, which made her job seem so huge to me. Her hair was always perfect, and her sleek suits with her fashionable high-heel pumps and pearls drew me to idolize her. She was my role model. As a young baby, there was a time when I lived with my Mimi and PawPaw while my mom divorced my father. My dad had served in Vietnam for several years. I was only two years old when they divorced, so I don't really remember too much about him during that time.

I was blessed to have two grandmothers and two great-grandmothers. Grandmother Perdue (my dad's mom) was a homemaker. My dad was the youngest of seven children and a 'late in life' child, so Grandmother Perdue was much older than my Mimi. My mom had me when she

was 17, and my Mimi was young when she had my mom. It was awesome to have both role models to look up to. I felt like my life was complete as a young girl because of my amazing grandparents. The only one I didn't know was my Poppy Perdue. He passed when I was an infant, so I don't remember him, but I heard he was an amazing man.

I did not see Grandmother Perdue often, but when I would visit her for the weekend, she would make me homemade bread. Her home always smelled of delicious food. She had a garden, so we had fresh vegetables, and she canned them for the winter. She was always in the kitchen preparing for the next meal. She would also make dresses for me that matched hers, to wear to church. She added little details that made me feel so special. In that era, she wore a broach with every outfit. I wish I still had the broach she gave me when I was a little girl. It was a dainty and gold in the shape of a bow with a small pearl in the center.

I really loved listening to Grandmother Perdue's stories. She would tell me about picking cotton in the field when she was a child. They did not have cars in that day. I was so fascinated hearing about her generation. Grandmother Perdue was a rock to me, despite the fact I saw her infrequently. I remember her as a solid lady. Like my Mimi, she was a hard-working woman who made a home with her consistent love and acts of kindness. My dad would send cassette tapes home with her that he had recorded for me to listen to. When I came to her house, I would sit in her lap, and she would play the tapes. She would say, "Your daddy wants to say hi to you. Listen…" Then she would play a tape of him telling a story. I would ask, "Where is he? I can't see him." She told me he was in the Army and would be home soon.

I can still feel the warmth of the room I stayed in on Dalworth Street. There was a train across the street that I loved to listen to as I went to sleep at night. She always tucked me in and said generic nighttime prayers with me. It is a fond memory I still treasure, like her antique furniture and homemade quilts. She was such a wonderful lady, who really lived life to the fullest, and I am sure it was not always an easy one.

Grandmother Perdue attended a local Church of Christ faithfully. She always gave me Juicy Fruit gum at church to get me to stop talking. I have such fond memories of sitting on the pew listening to the beautiful harmony of voices. I can only remember a handful of times that I attended with her. Each time, she put a stick of gum in my little purse with paper and a pen. She planned well because she knew I would talk and ask questions otherwise. She handed me a hymnal to sit on my lap, and I took out my paper and pen to draw pictures. When my pictures were completed, and if I was good, I could then have my Juicy Fruit gum. I only had one stick, so I knew it was to be saved for a special time.

After church, Grandmother always prepared a wonderful meal. We had fresh vegetables and homemade bread. She also made a cake or pie when I was coming. Perhaps she had desserts all the time, but I felt special because that wasn't something my Mimi made often. Every holiday though, Mimi made the best pies and cakes. My two grandmothers passed on to me the legacies of a career woman and a fabulous homemaker. I am thankful for both. Even though I have

always had to work while raising my children, I also appreciated the woman who was able to stay at home and raise a family.

As a little girl, I loved people and had a natural, magnetic personality. I was a little free-spirited child who never shut her mouth. So many times I heard, "Kimberly Ann, please be quiet." My mind was creative, and I had so much hunger for adventure. It is amazing how we receive natural God-given personalities at birth, and then some traits are formed within us as we walk through the experiences of life.

Mimi and PawPaw bought a weekend ranch in East Texas, and I was excited when we traveled there for the weekend. It is where I discovered my tomboy side. I would chase lizards and hide in the woods and collect pinecones from the beautiful trees. The Ranch was a second home—a vacation cabin which only had one large room the size of a double-car garage and a front porch. The room had several beds, a propane stove for heat, and a camper stove to cook on. It was like camping, but in a cabin. My PawPaw had a dream of retiring there some day. There were no bathrooms, so we walked down a dark path by flashlight, making it a fun adventure to potty in an outhouse. The farm felt like it was at least 1,000 acres to me during that time. The pine trees were huge and beautiful. To this day, I have a love for pine trees.

I thought my grandparents were the richest people in the world. They owned two places—one in the city and one in the country. This suited me well because I believe my DNA must contain a little bit of city and just a touch of country. I love the country for its simplicity. I have always been an outdoorsy kind of girl. I loved that we had no TV there. I just played outside in the sand for hours. In the city we had schedules and places to be, and our days moved so much faster than they did at the farm. Adventure excites me because I never stop going, and I see opportunity all around me. I recognized my passion for adventure even as a child.

As I grew older, my Pawpaw taught me to drive his huge red tractor, which made me feel so grown up. We plowed the fields and planted various crops. I loved to drive anything. I sat on that tractor for hours after my PawPaw was done and pretended I could plow that field all by myself. PawPaw also loved old cars and had a couple he was restoring. I played in an old car that didn't run anymore, pretending to take road trips. I sat in the car for hours pretending to have my children with me, and we would go to many adventurous spots. I kept myself entertained easily and never needed interaction with other children in order to enjoy my world. I have been told I was quite a beautiful little girl with olive skin and baby blue eyes.

Even though my family was not active in church, I felt inspired to broadcast hope. At the time, I didn't know what that meant. Somehow I just knew I was destined to communicate to the masses and offer hope. I was so drawn to the Lord as a young child. It was like I could see Him in my future, I could feel Him.

Jeremiah 29:11 says, "For I know the plans I have for you, plans to prosper you and give you a good life." Philippians 1:6 says, " I formed you in your mother's womb." That was always a mystery to me. I've often thought about how amazing it is that before I was born into this world, HE formed me. I've questioned how He would know what choices I would make. How could He make it all work out? Later in life, I saw that the Lord was with me the whole way, the whole time, even when I did not have a clue who He was.

Chapter Two

GROWING PAINS

BEING FULL OF LIFE AND PERSONALITY HAS SOMETIMES WORKED against me. Since my mother gave birth to me when she was only a child herself, I grew up around her friends, a lot of young adults. And because my dad was away serving our country, and soon after he returned home from Vietnam they divorced, I lacked the structure of a traditional family.

At the age of three, my mother married again, and this is where my little world got turned upside down. I learned a very different kind of entertainment, and it wasn't a healthy one, particularly for a toddler. As a child, I had a gift of turning things around and making them alright, or so I thought. I learned to process pain and awkwardness internally and just roll with it outwardly. My mother's Husband #2 was always mad from what I remember. I know now that he was an alcoholic. I remember objects being thrown in anger by Dad #2. Subsequently, my mother cried a lot, and she always seemed sad. I watched her hard-sobbing cry, after I saw him hit her. The smell of alcohol was heavy in the house, and there were usually beer cans on the counter. Our house was frequently busy because they had so many friends over.

Many of Mom's friends would hang out with me. Mike was one of them. He and his older brother were long-time family friends and much younger than my mom. His parents and my grandparents were also friends, so Mike visited our home often. I thought he and his brother both were so handsome. They looked like my Ken doll. Mike used to sing and play the guitar, so I thought he was a rock star. Even at the age of three, I had a special admiration for him. His dark hair, beautiful brown eyes, and deep voice made him famous in my little mind. His brother was equally handsome and could sing as well. I think my love of music was established during this time. I would dance around the living room as they sang, pretending I was a rock star as well. I felt just as famous and a part of their band.

Mike was probably around 19 years old, maybe younger, when one night he stayed over. I can't recall where my mom was when Mike and I were sitting on the couch as he sang songs to me. I was sitting on his lap, and everything seemed okay to me. Eventually, Mike said "Okay, it's time for bed," and we ran to my room laughing along the way. My bedroom was small, but my bed must have been a full size. Mike tucked me in and began talking to me. I was very enamored with his charm, as I listened to his every word. He was calming to me.

Mike always seemed to be glad to see me when he visited, so I had no reason to be apprehensive of him. As I lay there, he began to rub my arms and told me how soft my skin was and what a beautiful little girl I was. I am sure I was probably giggling and smiling. I trusted him. He was nice to me. He kissed me on the forehead and continued looking into my eyes. The kisses started lingering and moving down my face, but because they were so gentle, I didn't realize something was not right. When I felt his tongue on my body and my mouth, confusion and fear set in. He kissed parts of my body that were supposed to be off limits.

This was the beginning of my dark days. I would one day learn of Mike's death in a horrible car accident. It wasn't too long after this incident in my bedroom, and I cried so hard because he felt like a family member to me. The sexual fondling only happened one time.

Mom's second marriage ended quickly, and she then married Husband #3 from Amarillo. I was four years old, and I remember the first house we moved into because I was allowed to decorate my room any way I wanted. My mom worked with a company, Home Interiors, and she was into decorating at the time. I chose to paint my room lavender. Purple was my favorite color, and still is one of my favorites to this day. My mother bought me frilly curtains with a bedspread to match. I think my carpet was even a shade of lavender. We had a huge backyard with large full trees and a cute front porch.

A few months after we moved in, Mom became pregnant with my little brother. It was exciting, and I recall the day in late August when he came into the world. My Aunt Jan and Nini Oliver (my great-grandmother) came over to stay with me. I couldn't wait to meet *my new baby*, as I perceived him to be. I didn't know at that time if it was a brother or sister; I was just so happy that there was a baby coming home. I was going to get to hold the baby and maybe even feed the baby. Mom named my brother CJ. He was a little premature, and I think he only weighed five pounds. When I got to hold him, I just knew I wanted to be a mommy someday. He was so cute, and I committed in my heart to always protect him.

My mom and new Dad #3 had an active social life. Their friends came over on weekends, and I would hear Elvis Presley pouring through the speakers. He was popular in my house, as was Neil Diamond. I think my mother was in love with him just like everyone else's mom.

My natural father entered my life again around this time, and I began to spend some weekends at his home. He had a new wife, and they had a son, too. So, now I had two baby brothers, only one month apart. I didn't see my natural father consistently, and I don't remember my time with his son Billy as much as I remember my time with CJ. In either of their homes, every time my parents would leave the room, I would sneak over to pick up one of my brothers so I could rock and hold them. I would usually get in trouble because the babies were normally sleeping. CJ didn't mind—I looked at him as my own little baby doll because he was so tiny. Having two babies in my life was exciting.

My new stepmother was very strict. I never felt like she liked me much. My dad did most of the cooking. And when he made liver and onions, which I didn't like it at all, I would wait for them to leave the room, and I would feed it to the dog. PD the dog never said a word, and he could always count on me to feed him when I didn't like something they cooked. I fed him often. They didn't cook like my mom and Mimi.

I was thankful I didn't have to go to my dad's too often because it was very different in so many ways. The menu was much different than my mother's, and I missed the love my mom gave me when I went to visit Dad and Stepmom. The décor was different, too. Overall, their house just didn't feel like my home. I believe I discovered deep feelings during this time and recognized the difference

one's environment can make. Cleanliness of a home mattered to me, even then. I noticed that the way a home was decorated affected my feelings of safety and happiness. For these reasons and more, I began to appreciate my mother's home. It was always clean, and the décor was inviting. At my mother's home, we had chores every Saturday morning. She would make a list, and I could not go out and play until my list was finished. At my dad's home, I didn't have a routine. My stepmom was not a homemaker. From my memory, she read a lot of books and watched a lot of TV.

Life began to change for me. I was only five and a half years old, but I don't really remember the things I did for fun during this time. I do, however, remember the adult activities. My mom had a friend named Cindy. I remember her because I thought she was so beautiful. She had amazing, long eyelashes, she was tan, and she looked just like a Barbie doll. I thought she was amazing, and I admired her. Mom and Dad #3 would hang out with her and other neighbors down the street and play board games and cards while us kids played outside.

This was a weekend routine—we always had company, or we went to the neighbors' homes. Everyone had children, and I was the oldest, so I learned how to be the entertainer for the kids, and probably the boss. The leader within me was being developed.

Dad #3 joined the police force as a reserve officer with my PawPaw. We had a police scanner in our home, just like Mimi's home. I always heard my PawPaw's name, "JW Parker, do you copy?" I could listen to the police chases for hours. I would play with my dolls while I listened to what was going on in the big world. I thought my PawPaw was saving all of us from the bad guys. A no nonsense man, my Pawpaw was my hero. He was very serious all the time. He drank coffee all the time, and he didn't say a lot. He loved blue grass music, and we watched old shows like "Gunsmoke" and westerns with John Wayne. There was one comedy he loved, "HeeHaw." The one thing I remember from the show was a line, "Hey Grandpa, what's for supper?" Isn't it funny how we remember little details from our childhood that mark us to the core? When I see older movies, I always think of my grandfather.

We lived on Proctor Street in Grand Prairie, and in that day and age, kids played outside until dinnertime. I had lots of friends, and there was always fun to be had. A streetlight in front of my house was base for our hide-and-seek games. We often played kickball in the middle of street, and we hopscotched for hours.

Dad #3 and I used to cuddle on the couch. He was very affectionate, and I laid with him often. He was the first dad for me that felt like a real daddy, which seemed to bring a sense of belonging to my little life. I think there was a football game on TV the first time he asked me to rub his back. So, I started to rub his back. He said thank you and gave me a quarter as a tip. It became our little game. Mom would often be cooking in the kitchen while Dad #3 and I were watching TV, and it felt like family to me. My wheels were turning because I made money when I did chores or rubbed his back, and I began to think, "Wow, I can make a lot of money!" He always rewarded me with money, and I gratefully saved all of it in the little bank I received one Christmas. I loved to watch the coins pile up, count them, and take them to the real bank in exchange for dollar bills. I really felt very wealthy as a child, and I learned the value of money and saving.

I continued to provide back rubs for him. He worked hard with the telephone company, climbing tall poles daily. When he came home, he was so tired. He always mixed a drink and was ready to relax, so my job felt very important. And I felt like I was building a big business with my important job. At one point, he brought me a device he said made his back feel better. It was a vibrating massager to be slipped onto the palm of your hand while massaging. One evening, I was using it on his back, and he was drinking.

He said, "Let me show you something," and he turned over onto his back. I was sitting on him like I usually did, with my legs straddled over him, and I turned around so that my back was facing him. He slipped the massager on his palm and said, "Let me massage you for a minute and show you how it works." He rubbed my back. My shirt was off, and it felt so strong on my chest, it even made my voice vibrate, which made me laugh and giggle. This was our time, and spending time with my daddy and making him feel good was fun—and I even got paid for it. He would also tickle me, and I would laugh uncontrollably. Our fun little game went on like this daily for a long time.

One evening he said to me, "It's back-rub time." I jumped up onto his back, and he lay on his stomach. I smelled the familiar fumes of alcohol and sensed he was in a very happy mood. I rubbed his back like usual, and then he turned over and said it was my turn. I straddled him as always, and he rubbed my back. Something felt different this time. As he rubbed my back, he asked, "Do you want to see if I can make you tickle?" and proceeded to explain to me that his massaging device can also make girls feel very good. His demeanor changed, and his speech seemed suggestive. Even though I didn't know what that meant at the time, I could still sense a shift.

He told me he could show me some secret things that would make me feel good, and he began removing my panties after massaging my body. I wondered what he was doing, but I trusted him because we had played this game so many times in the past. The massager made his fingers vibrate as he very gently brushed between my legs. He began to kiss my neck. I remembered in the movies how a beautiful actress would do this kind of kissing with her man. And

I played this game with my Barbie and Ken. As he continued rubbing my back and kissing me, I noticed that his private parts were enlarging. The massager felt good to me, however I wasn't sure what was happening. I remembered feeling like this with Mike, and all of this adult activity began to influence my innocent five-year-old mind. When I watched TV shows and saw the actors kiss passionately, I was excited that I knew how to do that too. It made me feel grown up.

As I got older, our sessions reoccurred many times, and then he began to take more action. One evening he came into my room and laid on my bed to talk to me. He told me how special I was to him and how much he loved me. I felt very safe with him at this point. Then he began to kiss me like Mike had. I remember the horrible taste of alcohol and cigarettes on his breath. He began to move down my body and kiss me everywhere, and I didn't understand why at some points I began to enjoy it. Dad #3 continued his sexual acts with me night after night. The sessions always progressed. At the time, as I remember it, I would feel excited that we were going to play a new game. He made it very adventurous, and I enjoyed his games. Because he told me that it was our little secret, it was like having a secret friend and fantasy life. Our games continued and in that year, I believe I learned how to receive and give oral sex. I believe I was six or seven years old. I remember feeling like I was all grown up and privileged to know how to do all of this. The feeling of enjoyment made it feel right, even normal. He always told me that I was special and that he loved me so much, so I really didn't feel alarmed until the anger came in much later in my life.

As this went on for years, I would sneak his massager into my room and hide it in my dresser. I began to use it while I was alone in my room. As time passed, I learned to bring myself to orgasm with it, and it wasn't long I before I could achieve orgasm using only my hand. Learning the art of self-pleasure left me spending more and more time in my room. I became obsessed with having time alone. I remember looking forward to bedtime. I wish I would have known then that what I was doing was not a healthy practice for a child. But I didn't know.

Outside of our secret life, our family appeared to be just like everyone else's we knew. We had a boat, and later motorcycles. We went camping; in fact, the lake was one of my favorite places. When we all spent time together as a family with my brother and my mom, everything seemed idyllic. I don't know how at that age I was able to successfully keep our secret life such a secret.

One summer I was introduced to my stepsister who came to visit for a month. I believe I only saw her twice prior to that because she lived in Michigan. I believe she was a little older than me. I don't remember a lot about her, however I do recall that she and I shared a bed. One night, I don't know how it started or who initiated it, but we began to act like grownups and kiss and do the things our dad had done to us. I only have one memory of an encounter like this with her. Much of that season of my life is blurred events, mixed with some distinct ones.

I loved going to Possum Kingdom Lake. My brother I would get pulled behind the boat on an innertube, and I later learned how to waterski there. Camping and waterskiing became favorite pastimes. We brought our dirt bikes with us, and I would ride through the woods. I loved adventure. We spent many weekends on the lake, and over time the secret sessions with #3 began to trail off. They became sporadic and would only occur out of the blue.

There was a boy on my block named Tracy, and he used to come over to play kickball and hide-n-seek. I thought Tracy was cute. He was a couple years older than me and the coolest guy friend I had. I might have been around eight. One day around dusk, I hid in our large doghouse during a game of hide-n-seek, and when he found me, he crawled inside. I asked him if he had ever kissed a girl open-mouthed, and he said, "No! That's gross!" Still, he acted curious, so I asked him if he wanted to. He said no.

Night after night, we continued playing, and my crush on him only grew. I wanted to kiss him so badly. Eventually, I finally talked him into kissing me, and I taught him how to French kiss, as we called it back then. As I continued to show him the ropes of kissing, my fondness for being with Tracy escalated. Soon after we began kissing, Dad #3 caught us. He knew what I was doing. I felt so scared because even though it was what he taught me to do, it had always been our secret game. *Maybe I am only supposed to do with him*, I struggled to understand. I saw the fierce look on his face, and I knew I was in big trouble. He yelled, "Get in this house!"

My stomach was in knots, and I knew I was going to get a beating. I was so confused as to why I would be in trouble, and I could only reason that it must be because I was doing this with Tracy and not him. As my legs trembled, I thought I was going to get sick. My mother came into the room and asked #3 what happened. He explained what he caught Tracy and I doing. So, my mother asked me, "What do you think you were doing Kimberly Ann?" I was so confused, and I suddenly realized that something was not right. If I told our secret, I would be in even more trouble. If I told them that I just wanted to kiss him, I would be in trouble for feeling that way. The inner turmoil burned and bubbled in my gut. I didn't know what to say.

Finally, after my mother scolded me, I told her this is what #3 does with me, so I thought it was okay to show Tracy how to French kiss. My mother was shocked and wanted to know what in the world I was talking about. I began to explain to her how #3 and I had been kissing—I didn't talk about the other stuff. She broke down and cried, which broke my heart. *I did something wrong*, I thought. *It's all my fault.* I wanted to stuff my words back into my mouth, and I wished I hadn't said anything at all.

Next thing I know, Mimi and PawPaw were at our house, and we had a family meeting. The conclusion was that I was eight years old and simply made up this crazy story to get myself out of trouble. I was known to be a little bit of a drama queen and very much a tomboy all in the same package. But still, in retrospect I can't understand how they thought an eight-year-old could make up such explicit stories. I know they were concerned about the family's reputation, and back then you just didn't talk about this sort of thing. Besides all of that, #3 was a police officer, too. Nothing was done about it, however, I now realized that something was not right with my time with Dad #3, and I sank further into a very dark season of my life. I was maturing while shrouded in so much confusion, not understanding what I had done wrong and how I could possibly upset my mother and family so. My life became somewhat foggy, and I don't have many detailed memories during this season.

We started attending church from time to time at a little Baptist church. Sitting there with my family, I sensed serenity and safety. I enjoyed going to church. I loved the music, and the pastor was very nice. I didn't understand the message so much or the King James translation of the Bible, but I loved the way I felt just being there. Now I know it was the presence of the Lord that I felt. I saw other families and admired their closeness. I witnessed the purity of their love for each other, and I craved it for myself. When I saw daughters with their daddies, I wondered if they had experienced the same thing I had with my dad, but their relationships seemed different to me. Their innocence seemed pure. The little girls had open, trusting countenances as they gazed into their fathers' faces. My heart sank because I knew my life was different. I attributed it to 'being special' because that is what I was told. Only now do I realize that I was special in a very bad way.

My grandparents moved to our family ranch in East Texas. We began visiting there often. I loved the ranch. Riding dirt bikes and tractors was all I did, and I explored all over their land. Their house was new, and I loved it. My PawPaw cut down many trees throughout the years. They were so beautiful, however he had a dream to do some farming and ranching. Their handful of horses and one cow became pets.

We had many family gatherings throughout the years, which always involved blue grass music and lots of laughter. On one particular weekend when I was young, my great uncle was visiting there too. He was always very nice to me. He played the guitar, and my grandfather played the banjo and harmonica. Such great memories, and they continued for generations… And then there was the dark side, too. My Aunt B, a homemaker, was my Mimi's older sister. They would bake and cook amazing meals together. My great uncle and aunt had a camper shell that sat on the back of their pickup when they would come to the ranch. My great uncle wore overalls and seemed much older than my PawPaw. He knew I loved driving my PawPaw's tractor around their 40 acres, and one day he said he would drive me to the other side. He got on the tractor and sat behind me. We drove for hours it seemed, me sitting on the front of the seat between his legs. In the middle of the pine trees, he stopped the tractor and began to fondle my very undeveloped breasts. I responded to his advance just as I did with Dad # 3. I must have been only eight or nine at the time. I remember just letting him do it, and he knew I enjoyed it. This one, as with all new encounters, began slow, and time would pass before the next opportunity came. And I knew it would come.

The next time we were riding on the tractor, and I believe it was later that same weekend, he began to fondle my breasts again. I enjoyed it and remember thinking we should go somewhere more private so I could take my clothes off. Maybe I was curious if it would be the same encounters as I had with Dad #3. He invited me into his camper on the back of his truck. I remember the excitement I felt. He took off my clothes and began to kiss my breasts and stomach, and soon his mouth went between my legs. He stayed there for a while, and I saw him put his hand on his private parts, and then he exposed himself. I had seen this before, so it wasn't new—just a different, and much older person. I was enjoying what he was doing and soon climaxed, and I watched him do the same. After that, every time my uncle was at the ranch while I was, we would repeat this process. I remember getting excited to see him, knowing we would find a way to sneak into the camper and be nasty together. He seemed to make me feel even better than my dad did. He was so much older, and that confused me even more.

After each encounter though, I began to think there must be something wrong with me. *How do these men in my life, who are all family, want to do this with me?* I began to feel ashamed and solidify in my mind that *yes, something is definitely wrong with me.* I was so young, but in my precious years of innocence, I was conditioned to believe this kind of activity was normal, and it continued. As I reflect and wonder how I survived this season in which I was preyed upon, I now understand that I mentally escaped. I would will myself to think of other things, pretend I was alright, and afterward seek new adventure in an attempt to separate myself from my real life.

As I grew, the differences between me and other girls seemed even greater, and I no longer believed that I was a 'special girl' as I had been told. As early as the third grade, my grades were failing, and I was always in trouble. I slipped into a deep depression. I had to repeat the third grade because I was so far behind. I had a hard time focusing on my school work, as revealed in my poor grades. A heavy darkness hovered over me. I took some of my mother's pills in an attempt to end my life. I was so confused. I didn't understand what was going on or why I felt that way. I don't even remember what happened after taking the pills, but I do remember going to the doctor a lot and having multiple tests run on me. I was sick at my stomach all the time and was overwhelmed with turmoil in my mind. To this day, much of my memory of this time is missing—and in its place, darkness.

Chapter Three

I KNOCKED OVER A GAS PUMP

As TIME WENT BY, I HAD SEVERAL SEXUAL EXPERIENCES, NOT intercourse, but rather acting out romantic movie scenes with a few teenage boys and even a few female friends at the same time. We were adventurous pre-teens with no supervision. This typically happened after school while our parents were still at work. I don't remember ever feeling it was wrong, maybe because at least now it was happening with my peers. I thought it was just what everyone did. In fact, having sexual experiences (though shy of intercourse) felt normal. It wasn't until I discovered that it really wasn't age-appropriate behavior, that I began to feel dirty and ashamed.

I had a new best friend named Sherry who lived down the street. It seemed she had the perfect family. Every Saturday morning she and her mom would go shopping; it was their routine. Her dad was such a hero to me. I looked up to him and thought, *this is what dads do. How come my dad is not this way?* None of my dads were like him.

I was always in trouble at this point in my life. My grades were poor, and my young life was spinning out of control. My mother always had pills in her cabinet that she took to make her feel better. I thought if I could take some of them, maybe I would feel better too. I don't recall how many I took one morning before school, but I passed out in class and was rushed to the hospital. It turns out, the medication I ingested had been Valium.

After that episode, I felt even more like a bad girl. My parents often said, "We just don't know what is wrong with you." So I thought *something must be wrong with me*. Somehow, I had suppressed the stint with Dad #3—and I just couldn't anymore. It was evident in my behavior that something was not right. I had to convince my family I was telling the truth all along. I don't remember how I convinced them, but I finally did, and suddenly my life was changed. I was shipped off to live with dad and stepmom. She still wasn't any more fond of me than before. Though my dad didn't live far from my mother, life was very different at Dad's.

My mother loved me; she created a home and provided structure. I was required to do chores at her house before I could play. My stepmom didn't have the same routine. Rather, she would lie in bed and read on the weekends, and chores were not a priority. I really missed the closeness that I had with my mom. I missed having a steady mother figure in my life. I tried to make the best of it. I would jam out to Rod Stewart and rearrange my furniture the best I could with what I had. My room was at the back of my dad's house. I didn't have pretty bed sheets or frilly curtains, and there was nothing feminine around the house, so I tried to decorate my space the best I could. I created all kinds of crazy things on my own to make it feel like home.

Life at my dad and stepmom's was different in so many ways. However, the social gatherings were the same—just a different people group. The couples my dad socialized with were older, and their children were older than me as well. At ten years old, I was one of the youngest in the group and had the freedom to get into whatever came my way. It came naturally to me to just go with the flow. It's how I functioned.

When we went to my parents' friend's house for adult card games, there was lots of drinking. Being the youngest among all the teenagers was cool to me. I developed a huge crush on Bobby, my friend Donna's older brother. He looked like Steve Perry, the lead singer from Journey. He had long hair and was so adorable.

It didn't take long until I was introduced to marijuana, and we were all getting high on a regular basis every weekend while our parents partied. I felt as if I was growing up fast. I certainly did not feel like the pre-teen my age reflected. I was already doing everything the older kids did. Mark, the guy next door was my age, and we went to school together. We often stood outside his window smoking cigarettes and pot. There was nothing sexual about our friendship, and I enjoyed that. I mostly had guy friends. I just seemed to fit in a boy's world better than I did with the girls my age. Mark was a sweetheart of a friend, and he is still in my life today. This season seemed to last for a long stretch in my life. I continued smoking pot and then experimented with other drugs. I felt very cool, and life seemed steady for me, though clearly not in a healthy way.

After moving in with my dad and stepmother, I met my first love, and his name was Mike. We met in the 5th grade, I believe. He had—what seemed to me—a traditional family, and I was attracted to his family life. Mike and I experienced so many different things together. I began to sneak out at night and take my stepmom's station wagon over to Mike's house. I never got caught, and I never wrecked the car, which still amazes me because at 11, I could barely touch the peddles. I learned to drive a tractor back at my grandparents' home, and I was allowed to drive on our dirt road, which was only two miles from Mimi and PawPaw's.

Mike had a pool in his backyard, so that summer we spent a lot of time swimming and sitting in his hot tub. We kissed and made out, but we never went all the way. Mike showed me what a better quality of life looked like. His parents provided a good life for him, and their home was so warm and inviting. It just felt like family.

Mike would ride his bike over to my house, and I would sneak him into my room where we would talk all night and snuggle. Neither one of us really knew how to go all the way, but we became best friends. One time we almost got caught. We heard my dad walking down the hall, so Mike slid under my bed. My heart raced with fear because I just knew he was going to find him. We weren't found out that night, but there came a time when my dad came into my room unexpectedly, and we were busted. My dad drove with us over to Mike's house to tell his parents what we had done. I was humiliated. Soon after, Mike and I could not see each other anymore. I developed a lot of anger at this time because I didn't have my best friend to talk to anymore. I didn't understand why they would do this to me.

In this season, I learned to run. I ran away from problems and escaped the life I had just to feel something different. I ran away from home and walked to the local shopping mall. It was the called the Forum 303 Mall. Ironically, later as an adult in real estate, I would have this building as a listing for sale. It's really crazy how things work out. It's especially ironic because I hid in the bushes that evening and imagined how I could make a home in this little space with trees around it. I was found and taken home, then scorned and grounded for running away. That wasn't enough to put a stop to my adventures though.

Eventually, I decided to take another little trip out my window. This time I went down to a neighbor's home. They were true hippies. I just loved them for their free spirits. I lived with them for three days, while I am sure my dad frantically looked for me. Lucy, the lady of the house, had long blonde hair. She was so beautiful. I loved her vibe of peace, love, and rock and roll. I listened to all the 70s rock music and got high with them. I felt I was living the life, even if it was short lived. Soon I was back home, back to the hell I was living at Dad's house. I missed my mom terribly. She had been hospitalized due to a breakdown. All I could think about was that I wanted her to come home, and I wanted to be back in her home with her.

The day she called to tell me she was home, I cried and begged, "Please, can I come home? I hate it here, and I miss you." My mother came and picked me up, and I returned to my home with my little brother. We lived there, absent of my stepdad, and I suddenly I had no boundaries. I had freedom to do whatever I wanted. I had made the cheerleading team by then and met my second love, David, our school's all-star quarterback. He and I were close. He was my first real love, and it was with him that I lost my virginity. We were the cutest couple, and always together.

A year prior, Dad #3 bought me a red Yamaha motorcycle, which I loved. It was an Enduro 100, so I could ride it on the street or on dirt. I rode that bike everywhere. One time my best friend Valarie and I made plans to ride to Duncanville from Grand Prairie to go to a party—that's approximately 15 miles! We snuck out of the neighborhood only to spot two police officers. We suddenly turned around and saw the lights chasing us. We darted in and out of back yards and seemed to lose them, but ultimately we were busted. They loaded my bike up and off to jail we went. I can't remember who we called—probably her mom—but somehow, we got out of jail, and my mother never knew until later. I had some connection in helping me get my bike out of the pound. I always seemed to find a way out of trouble. Maybe it was from all the years of watching "Leave it to Beaver" and admiring Eddy Haskell's brilliant problem-solving skills.

At 14, I went to a birthday party for Valarie as she turned 13. It's where I met Tammy. Like the three musketeers, Tammy, Valarie, and I became the best of friends. Tammy had a life very similar to mine in a dysfunctional home. She was sexually abused, and though parts of her story vary from mine, her life was equally as hurtful. Her mom was very abusive. Tammy was just as daring as I was. We both loved smoking pot. Her parents were police officers, so we had to be even more careful around them.

Valarie's mom was a hippy-mom and so down to earth. We all loved her, and she adopted us as her own. We were always at Valarie's home. She had an older brother who was very good looking and pop-ular. He was a drummer, and his band would set up in the dining room of their home. I loved watching them, as I have always loved music, but had no gift. So, we would gather at Valarie's after school and get high with the older kids.

I have so many memories with these two girls. Tammy ran away from home at one point, and we made plans to go to a concert. The police were looking for her as we were all riding around in Grant's car, a friend of Valarie's brother. Fear of the police was real to me, as my grandfather was still on the Grand Prairie force and Tammy's parents were Dallas officers. Still, there we were running and hiding from the police. We went to Valarie's home to get something. Tammy hid in the car and waited for us to come out. While we were in the house, one of Tammy's friends called and asked about Tammy. Valarie told him, "Yeah, we have her in the car, and we're leaving for a concert." This person then phoned her mom and gave up Tammy's location.

When we all walked out front to get back in the car, we noticed the police driving up the street. Tammy had noticed them too, and she knew it was 'game over'. She took the pot from Grant's car and put it in her purse because she didn't want any of us to get busted for it. The police found her hiding low in the back seat and pulled her out. They were very rough with her, slamming her onto the trunk, then handcuffing her. We are all friends today. Valarie and I walked with Tammy as adults when she battled brain cancer, then died at age 50.

As crazy as we were, we had such good memories of going to concerts and acting as if we ruled the world. I was usually the instigator of the group, but Tammy was always up for anything, and Valarie just went along. Valarie was the stable one of the three of us. She followed the rules and kept both of us from much trouble, I am sure. If parents needed to be lied to, I was always the spokesperson of the group. Valarie's mom saw through all of our antics and didn't really want her innocent girl hanging with us, but somehow I still won her over and became a part of their family. We remained close into out teens, going to parties, wearing each other's clothes, and making our hair 80s big. Tammy and I were the wild ones. We loved adventures and boys. Valarie somehow seemed to keep us grounded. She was the voice of reason that called to us when we flew too high.

I continued to sneak out at night. I took the car because the motorcycle was too obvious at night. One night the girls and I were supposed to meet up with some cute boys. I made a plan to sneak out with the car and pick them up. We set out like we were big girls, though I was only 14 at the time. We cruised down Main Street feeling very grown up. We saw the guys we were meeting, and they pulled into a gas station. I was trying to act cool with the music blaring, and we all had on rabbit fur coats, as they were popular in that era. As I pulled into the gas station, I misjudged my turn and hit a gas pump—and it fell over. I still cannot believe I didn't blow up the gas station. My heart was racing as my girlfriends and I jumped out of the car. They got into the boys' car, and I faced my challenge alone.

I walked up to the attendant and said, "Sir, I am so sorry. Let me get my information out of my purse." Then I got in the car and took off. I drove home so fast, trembling with fear, praying my grandfather wouldn't find out through police channels. I went into my house and crawled into my bed, believing I had made it. I laid in my bed, my heart thumping with fear, thinking at any moment the police were coming for me. Then I heard a tap at the window and cackling from the same two girls who had just left me. I jumped up! They told me to come on, that the boys had their car out front. And like an idiot, I did.

So off we go, out on the town again! We were smoking pot, and cranking up the music, and having a great time. Every now and then, we would drive down our streets to make sure there were no lights on at our homes. On the last drive by, we saw all the lights on at my friend's house. As we drove by, her dad recognized us in the car. We were busted. The boys pulled over and let us out, and I told the girls, "Don't say anything about the gas station."

Her parents walked me to my house, and made me wake up my mom to tell her what we had done. Nothing was said about the car we took or the gas pump I hit. My mom called my dad, and he came over. My dad noticed that their car had no dew on it and asked if I had driven it. I lied of course. But my dad felt the hood and knew from the warmth that someone had been driving it. I still refused to confess.

I continued sneaking out and doing crazy things. Angels surely surrounded me in this wild season of my life.

Chapter Four

A TEXAS WILD CHILD IN ARKANSAS

THERE WAS A SUDDEN LIFE CHANGE. AGAIN. MY MOTHER MET an amazing man named Ed, and they married. We moved to Eldorado, Arkansas. I was devastated to leave my friends in Texas. However, I was also excited because of the security I felt with Dad #4. He was a good man with family values. He was strict on me, but in a loving, healthy way. He did things I had only dreamed a dad would do for me. He bought me roses on Valentine's Day just like he did for my mom. He talked to me and treated me as his own daughter. He bought me my first car—the coolest red Pinto with a sun roof, full glass in the back, and it was only a couple of years old. It had an 8-track player, and I felt sporty.

We had a toga party for my 16th birthday, and Valarie came to visit me that month from Texas. Her mother didn't know I hung with college-age kids, or she would have never allowed her to come. In Arkansas, everyone my age was still roller skating and doing activities I considered juvenile. It was hard for me to act my age, as I was so much more mature, having had so many experiences with my friends in Texas. We had so much fun that summer, cruising the main drag in my Pinto, driving around the Sonic, being cool and flirting with boys. We went shopping and bought matching overalls, as they were in style then. I was always on top of the latest trends in fashion. My season in Arkansas taught me the balance of family and a small town, even though I was running with an older crowd.

Soon though, it seemed that my mother was unhappy. She said Husband #4 smothered her. By this time however, I had bonded with him and learned his rules and expectations, and I had developed a lot of respect for him. He was the first dad I had ever known who wasn't interested in anything but family life and providing for his family. I loved and admired him. He took me shopping often and treated me like his little princess. The day my mother announced we were moving back to Texas, I was angry. I was determined that I in fact was not moving back.

I had been dating a guy named Ronnie. He was older than me and had a Trans Am. Ronnie and I became close, and I believed I was in love. My mother was determined to move, and she would not let me stay unless I was married. Being the rebellious girl I was, I was determined to get my own way. At only 16, I married him for three months just to gain her permission to stay in Arkansas. And so, Mom moved back to Texas, and I remained in Arkansas with my new husband in our efficiency apartment. The three-month-marriage seemed like a lifetime. I felt suffocated, so one night after a nasty fight, I took off walking down the street with no idea where I was going. I just knew I could not live under that kind of control. We were both so young, I can't believe our parents even allowed us to marry. I walked and walked that night. I don't recall where I ended up, but at some point, I called #4, and he came to get me. I stayed in Arkansas a bit longer and landed a job at the First National Bank. I lied about my age and was hired to run the checks through a machine so they could be recorded on a reel-to-reel tape. I felt like an executive woman and so grown up. I rented an apartment with some friends, so I had to quit school to keep up with work and rent. I continued working until the bank discovered my age, and I was fired. I was so tenacious during this time that I still fought the idea of going back to Texas. However, my stepdad had moved on and was a little put out with me, as I didn't honor him like I should have. I didn't understand the gift of fatherhood he was giving me. Later in life, I called him to thank him for what he did for me. I was in survival mode back then and made very poor choices. Ultimately, I had no choice but to go back to Texas.

I moved back in with my mom, and she was living a wild life. She was frequenting the Country & Western night clubs with her friends and doing what hurting people do. I was miserable with my life, and I was angry to find myself back in a dysfunctional family yet again. My life started to spin out of control, and I didn't even realize it. I kept pushing the limits for more and more excitement and adventure in an attempt to normalize. I lived in survival mode and didn't even realize it. It was a very dark season. I know now that the Lord was with me, even when I had no knowledge of Him.

By this time, Tammy had a baby and Valarie was living with an abusive boyfriend. Our lives had grown apart. I started running with a new friend, and she and I began to go to the clubs. I had a fake ID and got in anywhere I wanted. We used to enter the Legs and Wet T-Shirt contests. I started winning and became really addicted to the attention. It was easy money—all I had to do was wear heels and dance and show off my great legs.

I felt alone and displaced and desperately needed to fill my emptiness with something. Naturally, I craved excitement to make me feel whole. I had made new friends who had no depth. I can't even remember their names to this day. The girlfriend I was running with suggested we try topless dancing, pointing out the money that could be made. So that is what I did. There was a club on Northwest Highway called The Caligula. I walked into the club and saw a hot tub on stage. There were beautiful woman in sexy outfits and elegant heels on smaller stages. They all looked like movie stars. It was exciting and appealing to me because it all seemed so glamorous. I immediately felt I had a chance to be someone. This was a place where I could belong.

The first time I danced, I looked and felt like a rock star with my big hair and all my makeup. My first set was a little more difficult than I had imagined though, as I couldn't bring myself to take my clothes off on stage. I felt almost innocent and shy, even though I wanted to do what the other dancers were doing. I cried inside because I couldn't muster up the courage to take it all off on stage. We wore

T-backs, which is basically thong underwear, and it is all the ladies would wear on their second song. I was tenacious, and I was determined to become the best dancer in the place. The next night, we took some quaaludes and had a few shots of alcohol—and every ounce of my inhibition was gone.

I studied the other girls and watched how they seduced the men with their bodies. The men were not allowed to touch the dancers. Police officers were standing around to make sure of that, so I felt safe. I mastered the skill, and I began to make around $1,000 a week. This kind of cash was huge to me. I invested my money into a better wardrobe and shoes. And when I bought a 1979 Corvette, I thought I had arrived at the peak of my life.

After a long season of this, I was introduced to methamphetamines, the drug of choice among the dancers because we could keep our weight down and gain tons of energy. Eventually, I was doing meth daily. Methamphetamine is a manmade mixture of chemicals that gave me a fake moment of energy, then I could stay up for days on the poison. My mind was so far gone, I don't know how I functioned during this time. It wasn't long until I became a heavy user. I was so strung out on drugs, I didn't realize how close to death I had come so many times. I overdosed a couple of times and didn't even know what had happened. I believe there must have been angels all around me holding me up. Before I knew it, I had lived four years lost in this lifestyle.

I had not seen my family in months…which somewhere along the way became years. I missed them terribly and had not even heard my mother's voice in what seemed like forever. I was bouncing from one friend's house to another. My life was totally out of control. I moved in with Donna and her husband, a friend of my dad and stepmom's, where I had first learned about pot. Donna was just as strung out on drugs as I was. I began dealing large amounts of drugs to support my habit. During my stay at Donna's, I almost died. I had to call my mom. Under the influence of so many drugs, I couldn't even say my name. Mom came and gathered my things and took me to stay at her place. I lived with her for a couple of weeks. I was grateful she rescued me, but the relief was fleeting because I couldn't stay with her in my condition. I was so desperate to have my mom or dad rescue me and make everything better, but life made it evident that I had to fight my own battles.

Being saved from myself and then enveloped into a close-knit, solid family was only a fantasy of course. The reality was that my family, though I loved them so, was broken and dysfunctional. I remained hungry for security and unconditional love and acceptance, but I was not being fulfilled no matter where I searched. God was with me, I just didn't know it yet.

Nor did I know Mom had married, yet again. Husband #5 was not that fond of me or my lifestyle. I understand now because he had two young children, Amanda and Ron. I am sure the very sight of me made him fearful of the influence I might have on them. After I moved on from Mom's new family, Valarie's mom rescued me. I was still strung out and dancing, but Lou helped me get straight. She and her husband Terry provided me a place to live, food, and safety. Lou and Terry had found God. They kept asking me to go to church with them. I was starving for something to fill me, however I was so heavily medicated, I couldn't feel God even though I went with them to church.

One Sunday, I walked to the altar and gave my life to God. I wanted a new life so desperately, only to leave church feeling very empty and hopeless. I was so messed up on drugs, I couldn't even feel what God was trying to do. I had never experienced unconditional love. I had always had to work for it, perform for it. It was so foreign to me, I didn't know how to receive it. So I kept on self-destructing. I lived with them for several months, then I moved on. This was probably one of the darkest seasons of my life. I continued to fight through it and never quit, but I I had no direction, therefore I was floating aimlessly on a sea of drinks, drugs, and destruction.

Under this dark cloud, an opportunity presented itself for me to help my friend Sam, who used to come into the club. Sam had an uncle from another country who needed a place to live. He was trying to get citizenship here in the States. Sam asked if I would split an apartment with his uncle. I had my own two bedroom apartment in Dallas. His uncle spoke no English and was the age of my father. It was my task to attempt to teach him English and how to learn to live in the US. The arrangement only lasted a couple of months, as I was not in the mental state to teach anything to anyone, and not being able to communicate with him left me with no patience.

Chapter Five

GROWING A FAMILY TREE

O NE WEEKEND, WHILE STILL WORKING IN THE CLUB, DESTINY opened a new chapter for me. I met the man who would become the father of my children. Joel came into the club and sat down. He was a rock star to me, and a kindred spirit. We both loved music, and he was so easy-going. We sat and drank the whole night. After closing, he and I went to eat and do what we did in that sort of life, and we talked all night.

He was a musician, and his band was really good. He often had gigs down the street from where I worked, so I would go watch him play. I loved the way he made that guitar scream. I dreamed at that time he would become a rock and roll star, and I'd be a rock star in my own world. Since he was a musician and most of his events were in the evenings at various clubs, he kept the same hours as me. So, we would hook up after both of our gigs and stay at his place. Joel and I became very close. We even looked alike—both of us with our big, long hair. He was my own Eddie Van Halen. Eventually, Joel and I moved in together. Joel was good for me in so many ways. For the first time, I felt I had a best friends who had my back. I stopped the hard drugs. Just stopped! I don't even remember going through withdrawals. His example of not destroying your body with the poison I was taking was good for me.

Joel had a great family. His mom and dad lived in New Mexico, and they supported his dreams. His father paid for his school and gave him money to live on. He was attending a guitar conservatory school, and then he went on to North Texas State where he studied jazz and various types of music. He seemed to have the grounding I was always hungry for.

It wasn't long until I became pregnant with our first son, Sean, which meant dancing came to an end soon after. Becoming a mother caused so many emotions to arise, and I began to long for my family. I wanted to share the news with them, even though I knew I had not been living right and they would be disappointed in me. I felt very ashamed and nervous, but I made the call and went home to see my family and introduce them to Joel.

Finally, my family and I were reunited. Everyone loved Joel, as he was a musician, and we always had guitars, banjos, and other instruments present with all of our musical friends. I wasn't showing yet, but the news of my pregnancy was well received. Everyone was excited! They were probably frightened too, wondering what I was going to do with a baby. I was grateful they all loved Joel. Who wouldn't? Joel never met a stranger. He was warm and laid back, and they saw my love for him. He was a good man. I was very excited to be having a baby of my own—and I was also totally frightened. I landed a job at Lord and Taylor in the cosmetics department representing Lancôme. I loved the job. My life seemed to be settling into a normal that I wanted.

Sometime later, we were at Mimi's house visiting for the weekend. I was six months pregnant, and my PawPaw had just passed away in December. My PawPaw was my rock, and his death marked me in a way I didn't expect. I didn't get to the hospital in time to say goodbye to him. My Mimi was hurting. His death came with no warning; he was only 58 years old. I watched my Mimi pick up the pieces and keep going.

Mimi worked for the Justice of the Peace, and she told Joel and me over coffee that I needed to be married before I had the baby. We were all healing over PawPaw's death, and in my heart wanted to please her. We married that day in the clothes I had on. I didn't have a ring or anything. We just got married at Mimi's house that day, and I knew she was happy that her first great grandchild would be brought into this world with a mom and dad who had the same last name. I was truly happy and very excited that life was looking so promising. In the core of my heart, I craved connection and belonging, and I felt I had found that with Joel. After all, we were married now. Later he did

get me a ring and I felt married at 22 years old. I was carrying his child in my womb, and that excited me!

Being pregnant was so natural for me. I had no problems and wanted to have a totally natural birth. I found a doctor who believed in that method. The due date came, and the baby didn't arrive, so I began to walk each day that passed and subscribe to nearly every myth that promised to speed up delivery. I was seven days past due, and felt like I would pop at any moment. After another week with no baby, I finally took a tablespoon of castor oil and went into labor that night. I'm not sure if that was the kicker, or if it was just time for my little bundle of joy to arrive.

Joel, Jr.—also known as Sean—was born March of 1986, almost 9 pounds and 19 inches long. I didn't realize it until I was in the moment of birthing this child, but this is the only time in a woman's life that she cannot change her mind. The pain started, and it was a little overwhelming. I remember thinking, *NO! I don't want to do this*. I was only 22 and didn't realize how much pain I would endure. Halfway through the labor, I was pleading for something to ease my pain. But I had signed an agreement to endure the birth naturally, and that is what I did for 17 hours. Once Sean was born, I looked down at his little face, and tears ran down mine. He was so perfect. I fell in love with him instantly. No greater gift had I ever experienced.

I took him home, and I was scared to death. My mom came home with me, and when it was time to give him his first bath, I picked him up so gently and put him in his little tub—and he screamed. My mom took over because I thought I was hurting him. She just bathed him and swooped him out of the tub and slathered him in lotion. Everything was natural to her.

I wanted to nurse him, but I was having such a hard time getting him to latch on. So then I became fearful that he was not getting enough food. But once this child learned to latch on, he never forgot. I loved being a mother. Sean was the joy of my life. As time went on, motherhood agreed with me. I spoiled this child with so much love. I adored him. My son.

Life for Joel moved forward with his band, but my role had changed significantly as a new mom. I didn't go to all the gigs anymore, and Joel and I began to grow apart. I wanted to be a mother and create our family tree, all the while Joel was still chasing his dream of becoming a famous rock star. He was an extremely talented guitar player, and I believed in him. Still, after years of supporting his dream while simultaneously doing all we could in life as young parents, things began to change.

We had no tools to improve our fragile marriage. Neither one of us had a solid perception of what a healthy marriage should even look like. Though he had a much better home life growing up than I did, we were both young and living for the moment hoping Joel would land a record deal and life would be great. Joel did come close; he made a couple of albums and did very well. He was even one of the Texas Tornados, a distinguished award for being one of the top ten guitar players in Texas. I was very proud of him. But our marriage didn't make it. Joel and I were just so young and neither of us had the skills we needed to navigate through my emotional pain and his unique lifestyle as a musician. We were immature in our early twenties with some difficult challenges to face. I was so hungry for truth and stability in a time when very little seemed certain.

After leaving, I did what most single women do. I hit the bars, started drinking, and sought attention. My biological father lived close to me and had come back into my life. He kept Sean for me when I went out to party. About two weeks in, I kept getting sick. I just knew I had an ulcer or something wrong with me, only to find out I was pregnant. I went to Mom and Dad #5, and they gave me money to have an abortion. They thought it would be too hard on me to have another child with Joel and I being freshly separated.

I was working for a large insurance company at the time, and I went to my boss, Sharon. I sat down in her office and began to tell her about my situation. I started to cry when I told her I needed to take some time off to have an abortion. She looked at the broken woman I was sitting in front of her desk, stood up, and shut the door. I will never forget what happened next. It was the first time in my life I felt another presence in the room. I felt God.

Sharon sat back down at her desk, and I felt something in my life was about to change. She said to me, "Kimberly, God makes no mistakes, and this baby is a gift to you. This baby has a destiny, and you have a destiny."

I told her, "I understand what you are saying, but God does not know me. I have never been to church, except for a few times as a young child."

She responded with something that intrigued me. She said, "Kimberly, He knows the number of hairs on your head. He has a plan for you."

The thought of a God, who created the universe, knowing *me* really excited me, and I felt a love come over me like I had never felt before. In my limited experience in life, it was like finding out a celebrity knew me or was related to me somehow. My head was spinning by this time, and tears ran down my face. I found myself unexpectedly in wonder at what this discovery could possibly mean for my life. Sharon told me I could have the time off.

I had to leave for the day because I was overcome with emotion and a bewilderment at what I believed could have only been the presence of pure Love—of God—right there in Sharon's office behind closed doors. On the long drive home that day, I pondered what had just happened as well as what the future might hold. I began to think about Sean and the idea of having another baby. I thought of how hard it would be to raise two children alone. I was terrified at the thought. As I gave thought to everything Sharon had just told me, I kept wondering if it was really true. Still, I could not let go of the feeling I had just experienced, the love of GOD and the idea that He actually knew me, even though I didn't know Him.

I began to think about my past and all the things I had done that people who go to church wouldn't approve of...my dancing, the drugs, and the way I dressed for starters. But I was determined to find out more about this God who already knew me. When I first began to go to church, I could feel many of the women's judgmental eyes. I did not look like a church girl because I wasn't, but I wanted to be. I constantly felt like I was trying so hard to fit in where I didn't appear to belong—but I knew I was supposed to be there. I was so *hungry* to know God. I wanted so deeply to experience the love everyone spoke about, the love I felt in Sharon's office. I wanted to experience for myself. Gratefully, my hunger led me to people who were real, genuine, and neither critical of my appearance or my past.

I began to think about a sweet friend, Wendy Knaack, who I had worked with at Cigna. She and I could have passed for sisters. In fact, people often asked us if we were. Wendy invited me to her parents' Christmas party one year. They had a beautiful home with the largest Christmas tree I had ever seen. Their home was so warm and full of love, and I remembered how much I had admired the relationship

Wendy had with her mom and dad. Her dad was a pastor. The thing I loved most about Wendy was that she was so positive, and she always encouraged me. I thought about her as I pondered the idea of God knowing me. I thought of the connection she had with her parents, and how I had felt the same kind of love in their home as I had in Sharon's office, and I began to cry. I yearned for that kind of love in my heart. I wanted it so badly, but I didn't know how to get it.

That evening, I took a bubble bath with a glass of wine and decided I was going to have the abortion, and I could sort out the rest later. Going to bed having determined my course of action, I slept like a baby. When I awoke the next morning, something had changed. I felt overwhelming joy about being a mother, and I fell in love with the baby I was carrying. I immediately decided not to have the abortion. I called Joel and told him I was pregnant. He came right over and we talked. He cried, and I cried, and we decided to get back together.

I shared with him my experience with Sharon. I told him what she had said, but how I had decided the night before to just get an abortion and not tell him. And I described the inexplicable change of heart I felt when I awoke that morning. We had a deep conversation about everything, and I began to feel hope. I told him I wanted to start going to church, and I wanted him to quit the band and commit to fatherhood and marriage. So, Joel enrolled in a technical school, and I believed we were on a path that really gave our marriage and family a chance to survive. He worked hard at school while working full-time at his job. We both accepted God as our personal savior and were baptized together. This was the happiest day of my life. We were creating the family and place of belonging I had always wanted.

Life was going well, my belly grew, and I just knew I was having a little girl. I carried this baby differently, and I just felt like it was my girl. I named the baby Tiffany Danielle, and I was seeing pink everywhere. After a few months, I learned that my little girl was not a little girl after all—my second child was a boy. It only took a minute to wrap my head around the news, and I was just as excited! I did well with boys, as I grew up with brothers and already knew the boy world well with Sean.

When I was six months pregnant, Joel asked me to go to a party with him and his friends from work. I told him I didn't really want to go because I knew they would all be drinking and who knows what else. He said, "I have done everything for you. I quit the band, and I am going to school, as well as working full-time. Can you please go with me on this?" I relented. We walked into the party, and as any outgoing wife, I began to introduce myself and mingle. It wasn't long before I knew I didn't belong there. The people there were doing things that I wanted to get away from. I watched everyone get totally wasted. I was devasted, as I was fighting my way into a new life and had invested every ounce of hope into this new pregnancy and new start with Joel.

We finally left the party. I left him sitting in the car, and I went upstairs to our apartment. I don't know what time he came upstairs. It was Saturday, and I had plans for us to go to church the next morning. I got ready for church, as had become our routine on Sunday, but he was passed out. I didn't wake him. I went to church on my own and cried through the whole service, begging God to please help me. I thought my marriage was going to be better now, but instead I saw the residue of my past—of our past. When I got home from church, he was sitting on the couch watching football. I walked through the door and went straight to my room.

He came in and asked me, "What is wrong with you?" I thought to myself, *Really? You are kidding me right now!* He was clueless about what had happened the night before. I know he thought I still rolled like old times, but I didn't. I knew then, things were probably not going to change. Months went by and Joel continued going out with his friends. One night he came home covered in hickeys. That was it for me. I was done.

We continued living together while we waited for our second boy to arrive. I was very excited to meet my new son. My miracle child. On Easter, I was so huge and ready to have this baby. We had gone to an Easter egg hunt for Sean, and we played all day at the park. It was a fun family day. Later that night, or rather in the early morning hours, my labor began. It was time. We grabbed the suitcase and took off to the hospital. I had already decided—this time I want the epidural.

Nine hours later Jered Parker came into the world. Mom, Mimi, and I had already decided he would be named after his grandfathers. Jered Harlan and JW Parker. He was so adorable. I would discover that he was not quite as easy as Sean was when it came to sleeping. Jered was a little more high maintenance, but adorable nonetheless.

Six months later, the last sliver of hope that my marriage may work vanished. I released the fight for my marriage, and decided I could make it with God. I filed for divorce and began a new chapter in my life. It was a breaking point for me, a marker in time that the life I once had would never be the same. Pain and the fear gripped my heart. I did not understand what I was feeling, but I knew I was the only one who could make a healthy change for my boys and myself. I felt a sense of destiny in the midst of the darkness. I felt hopeful that everything would work out for my good. Eventually, I would be okay because I was determined that better days were ahead of me.

Chapter Six

NEW LIFE, OLD GHOSTS

CONTINUED ATTENDING THE SMALL BAPTIST CHURCH WHERE JOEL and I were baptized. I was the only single woman in attendance. I felt so alone and broken. I had no idea how a woman should carry herself in church, nor did I understand how one should dress. My heart was brimming with love for God, however my growth and maturity were slow to follow. My dresses were shorter and my make-up was bolder than any other woman there. Suddenly single, I felt like an outcast, rejected. The looks the other women gave me made me feel shame, even though it could have been unintended. They didn't know where I came from or the triggers I had. I didn't even understand the trigger of shame. Their responses to me made me feel as if I was a threat to them, when I truly just wanted to learn about God and be accepted among friends.

One of the male leaders of the church gave me a Living Bible as a gift. He must have noticed how green I was. Since I had never been in church as an adult, I didn't know the scripture or how to find references quickly. I purchased tabs from a local Christian bookstore to mark the names of the chapters. I could not get enough of the Word. Another gentleman offered to help me learn how to study God's Word. I believe his heart was pure—I never felt any underlying motives from him. Still, neither did I know the boundaries and dangers of a married man speaking with a single woman. I accepted his offer and began to have conversations with him on the telephone about the Word. He taught me how to look up references that were in the footnotes. The Bible came alive to me. I couldn't get enough of it. I was growing with God and learning what being a follower of Christ was all about. It began to feel like a treasure hunt as I connected the stories with the meanings. God was showing me a new world and how to live a Christian life as the Bible began to make sense to me.

After a few study sessions with the male leader by phone, I received a phone call that crushed me. His wife called me to tell me it was inappropriate for me to be talking to her husband, and she wanted it to stop. I was devastated. My heart was pure and very innocent. Now that I am older and more mature, I understand. But in the moment, I felt harshly judged and misunderstood. I knew my heart was in the right place, but once shamed, I left the small 50-member congregation. Defeated by her beratement, I questioned whether I was good enough to be a child of God.

I found a larger mega-church that offered a singles ministry. I wanted to know all the rules of the church and belong without feeling singled-out and shamed. Going through a divorce was not easy, and I felt I needed to be embraced by other singles and likeminded people. I missed Joel and the family we had.

Though I didn't recognize it in the moment, in retrospect I know we were just so young and didn't know how to get help. Over time I began to realize that when life got hard, I ran. When I felt the slightest ache of abandonment, I fled the scene to avoid the pain. I came to regret this instinct so many times as I grew with the Lord.

After I joined the largest Baptist church in town, and I was excited again. I was new there, and no one knew me. It felt like another fresh start. I joined the singles group and began to learn how to serve my church. This church offered me hope with all their programs and avenues for discipleship. What's more, I fell more deeply in love with the Lord because I was growing and understanding His Word. I was eager to keep learning about God's Word and be closer to Him. After a couple of years though, I felt like there was something deeper, something I hadn't tapped into maybe. I was a seeker.

I became friends with Kevin. He had a friend named Steve. And Steve introduced me to a Spirit-filled church. Walking into the sanctuary, I immediately sensed something different. Worship was different. At my very first visit, I noticed people were expressing their love to God by raising their hands during praise and worship. The sight of their freedom to worship amazed me. I sat there, hoping I could learn to be free enough to lift my hands too. It took me a while to get them all the way in the air, but every service I practiced until the freedom to love God recklessly and fully enveloped me.

Worship became an important part of my life, and my friend, Steve, became more than a friend. I fell deeply in love with him. He was a worshiper and so handsome and GQ. I believe God demonstrated to me through Steve what it was like to be adored. I learned that someone could love me just for me and not for what I could do for them. He was such a Godly man. We were both single parents of two children. His son was my son Sean's age. We began to date, and life seemed to be turning around for me again.

Steve taught me how to have clean fun in life. He made the sweetest gestures to show me day after day that he truly loved me. He wrote me sweet notes all the time and brought me flowers. He prayed for me each time our day ended and called me every morning and prayed over my day. He would even sing me worship songs and leave them on my voice mail. *Who does that?* Wrapped in this perfect love, a fierce fear reached up from my belly and gripped my heart. Everything was so perfect that I began to wonder if it was real. *Is this what true love is really all about?* My emotions began to spin out control. I couldn't figure out why I was so afraid all the time. I wanted to love him freely because I adored this man, but the doubts would not leave me alone. Every one of my doubts stemmed from the paralyzing fear he would abandon me like every other man in my life had before.

Ultimately, I broke it off with him. My heart was shattered, but not by his doing. Understanding that I was out of control again, I began to search for counseling. I was so eager to understand what was wrong with me, to know why I could not let someone love me. During my years of mental and emotional development, I experienced so much pain, and distortion, and confusion that fear had become comfortable to me. When fear was absent, I had foreboding thoughts that it was just waiting to pounce on me again and take my security and happiness from me. So, in an effort to protect myself, I tried to beat it to the punch. Determined to figure out what was wrong with me, I found a great counselor who helped me talk through things. Even then, I didn't fully understand the depths of the pain I carried from my childhood. As a result, I walked through life in constant confusion. I missed Steve and felt like I hurt him because… I did. In the end, he probably thought I was crazy.

I was working in the travel industry, and I had just turned 30. My boys were so young, and I wanted to provide them a stable home life. I desired to purchase a home but didn't know how I could possibly pull it off. Both boys were in sports. Sean played coach-pitch, and when they lost their coach, I stepped in and coached his boys team. My life was all about my boys. God provided a way, and I purchased a home for us. My boys' grandfather, Joel's dad, gave me the money for my closing costs, and I purchased my first home for $78,000. My payments were $700 a month—and I was terrified. It had just gotten real for me that I was an adult.

I loved our home though. I nested and decorated it to be a warm, safe place for us. It was roughly 1400 sq ft with three bedrooms and two baths, lots of windows that provided natural light, and a large wooden deck on the back of the house. It looked like a beach home, just without the beach. I treasure the entire experience. It was the first time I saw the Lord work out all the details when I stared them down and didn't have a clue. I had no idea how to go about purchasing a home. But God did.

I enrolled the boys in private school at our church. Sean was in elementary, and Jered was in daycare while I worked. And my counselor continued to help me uncover new things. I discovered that many concepts and principles I had adopted as truths in life were actually not true at all. My belief system was built upon the shaky foundation of pain and fear that had been constant in my life from the beginning. I had not yet resolved, or been set free from, the paradigms I knew as a child and young adult. For example, I learned the rules of the church included 'no sex outside of marriage.' But in my first three decades of life, sex had made me feel loved, so I was a little confused. And I was terrified to make a mistake. My expectations for myself were to get things right and be perfect—a total set up for failure.

In 1995, Lou and Terry, Valarie's parents, were working through a program called Pathways, and they wanted me to go through the program too. Pathways was developed by Phil McGraw, later quite famously known as television's Dr. Phil. I began the program in 1996. It was a four-month commitment and the hardest journey I had ever made emotionally. "The Weekend" as they call it begins by breaking down the walls of your heart. I was so scared as I worked through the program, however, quitting was never an option for me. I believed I would be set free from my dark pain that no one really knew about or understood. I didn't even understand it. I just knew it was a heavy piece of luggage I carried everywhere I went—better description would be a ball and chain that clung to me.

At the time I completed the Pathways program, participants attended The Weekend, then eight days later they attended The Walk, which was essentially their version of Boot Camp to deal with your stuff. I was full of fear and anxiety, however I was ready to do whatever it took to be released from my past. I desperately wanted to be a free woman. One exercise in particular hit me hard. It was a visual journey in my mind that opened my eyes as to why I so often felt insignificant, lost, and ashamed. The room was dim as the facilitator talked us through the instruction. It went something like this…

"You are walking down a narrow path in the forest. You notice the beauty of the trees and the smell of the flowers and nature…" I could see it. It was beautiful, and I continued to listen and actively engage as the facilitator continued taking us down the path. He said, "There is a door ahead of you, and two people are standing there. Walk toward them." I did. "When you get to the door, you see it is your mom and dad standing there. What do they look like?" I looked and saw two human figures. The figures had no faces. They were just bodies with heads of hair, but their facial features were completely absent. It was very strange, and I asked the Lord what it meant. Meanwhile, the facilitator continued and asked us to look at ourselves. "What do you see?" I cried because I saw a beautiful little girl who looked like an orphan. I had the Thumbelina doll I had loved as a little girl under my arm. My hair was matted, my face was dirty, my little dress was tattered and worn, my shoes were scuffed up, and my little socks were dirty. Seeing this image of myself was devastating, as I had always strived so hard to look nice and be in fashion, but the child I saw as myself was an orphan child.

The exercise revealed to me that I felt like an orphan, even though I had an amazing mother who loved me. She was walking her own path alongside me, and she did the best she could. My mother was always my biggest cheerleader, and she believed in me. Truly, love does cover a multitude of shortcomings. So why did I feel like an orphan?

After several exercises we did throughout the week, the Day of Contract came. The Pathway program was designed like an onion, the intent being to peel back the layers of your heart to reveal your authentic pain. The whole process led up to Contract Day, when I would deal with my issues and make lifelong commitments to myself for my path forward. I was numb, not knowing what to do with all the emotions I had uncovered throughout the week. During our journey, the TA's (Training Assistants) made notes about each attendee and then assigned each of us to a small group with a TA to lead us. Because I shared with them about my Daddy #3 and my biological father, they helped reveal something I had never thought of.

It was a moment of truth. I had never confronted my stepfather and told him that what he did to me was not okay. I had not forgiven him, and in fact I didn't really feel anything toward him. I just moved forward in life with indifference toward him. In the small circle, our TA asked me why I thought it was okay that he did those things to me.

I responded, "Well, it isn't okay. It's just what happened, and it is in the past. Who cares anymore? I am an adult. I am over it."

She pushed a little harder and put a man in the circle and instructed me, "Kimberly, this is your stepfather. Tell him what he did to you was not okay and that he hurt you." The crazy thing was this man had Daddy #3's eyes, almost identical, and I broke down and cried so hard. I couldn't talk to him. Still, they all pushed me. "Tell him, Kimberly."

Finally, I softly told him, "It's not okay."

The TA challenged, "Really, Kimberly? This man took your childhood and thought nothing of it. And you are going to passively tell him that it was not okay? Kimberly, get pissed, and TELL HIM!"

My heart was pounding out of my chest. I finally got angry and yelled at him. I beat a pillow and cried my heart out. I yelled, "You stole my innocence! You took something I can never get back!" After bawling my eyes out, it actually felt good to stand up for myself. I felt empowered. As a child, no one made a big deal of it when the abuse was exposed, so I believed it didn't matter and that I was not important. *Just ignore it and move forward.* That's the message I got.

After the Pathways exercise, I became brave. When I got home from The Walk, I called #3 and confronted him over the phone, as he lived in a different city than me. The minute I heard his voice, I began to quiver all over. His response to my call was a further shock. I told him, "What you did to me as a little girl was not okay. I felt so used because you did all the right daddy-things for my brother, but I was only a sex toy to you. It was not right."

He cried and told me he was sorry.

I forgave him. I told him about the program I was going through and that this call was necessary for my healing and for me to move forward to live a healthy life. I truly forgave him, and it felt amazing.

I finished the program and then went into training to become a TA. I did this for several years. Being a TA is a volunteer position, and I had to coordinate care for my boys so I could be away from them during my training. It was so worth it to bring my healing full circle and to then affect the lives of others who were hurting. The program was truly a game changer in my healing process and shaped me into the strong woman I have become today.

Chapter Seven

CREATING ROOTS IN THE WORD OF FAITH

TIME PASSED, AND I BEGAN WORKING IN THE MARKETING department of a travel company. I combined travel partners for consumers which included air, car and hotel deals. I was in charge of the Central United States, which put me in the air at least once a week. When I traveled, I listened to ministers on tape and any spiritual teaching I could find to feed my faith.

This is when I discovered a woman who would later become my hero. Joyce Meyer has a story similar to mine, and many of her stories are identical to mine. I purchased every one of her tape series I could get my hands on and listened to her messages over and over for years.

Another dynamic spiritual giant, TD Jakes, had just started a church near my home, so I began attending church there. He had just written a book, *Woman, Thou Art Loosed*. He held a conference just after the release of his book where I was healed even further. I loved his church. As a white woman in a black minister's church, I was a minority, but the worship music and the freedom with which the black culture worshipped God taught me to be bold with my worship as well. I truly loved the various textures and layers that existed in one church when all of the races came together to praise God. Jakes was the most in-depth preacher I had ever heard. He has revelation on the pain women go through. I will never forget one message he preached called "Find Your Brand of Person." It has stuck with me for years. I attended every service I could and watched athletes like Deion Sanders and Emmitt Smith get saved. I was literally sitting ten feet away when Deion gave his heart to the Lord. It marked me.

My journey of healing and empowerment continued as I devoured every teaching I could listen to in the car in between sales calls to my clients. And after I put my boys down for bed at night, I watched my favorite ministers on TV. The dream was growing within me. A thought process started in me about Joyce Meyer. *If God used her and her story to help me, what if I could help someone else with my story?* I began to feel the call on my life to minister. Joyce was my mother's age, and in a completely different phase of life than me. I was a single mom with two boys, and I didn't see how in the world I could accomplish this feat. One day, mopping my kitchen floor, I envisioned myself teaching other women just the way Joyce Meyer was doing it. The dream was in my heart, I just didn't know how God would use me and my story to encourage others.

I saw another minister, Casey Treat, on Christian TV one day. I believe his program followed Joyce Meyer's. He talked about knowing your God-given destiny. He had a book in print, so I ordered it. Being a tape junkie, I got his tapes as well. I spent years listening to the teachings of different ministers.

I wanted to go to Bible School, but being single, I didn't feel I had the support or the strength to do it all. I found out about a faith conference called The Believers Convention right where I lived in Fort Worth, Texas. It sounded great, and I wanted to learn about faith—after all, I would need faith to move mountains if I were going to accomplish everything God planned for me. As I made plans to attend The Believer's Convention, I also searched for a Bible School to attend. Casey Treat's school was in Washington state. I just could not wrap my head around moving us there with no savings whatsoever. I owned a home now and had a mortgage. I also had two boys who depended on me. *How can I do this?*

I attended the Believers Convention for the first time and was introduced to the ministry of Kenneth Copeland, Dr. Jerry Savelle, Jesse Duplantis, and Creflo Dollar. Walking into the exhibit hall where all the ministers display their products was an experience. I was intrigued by the possibility that I could do this. I was amazed at the level of faith these people were teaching. Kenneth Copeland became my hero of faith, and then I learned about other faith teachers like Kenneth Hagin. Dr. Savelle became another favorite because he was a gentle father. He had two daughters whom he spoke of often, and it was clear he adored his girls, Jerriann and Terri. I began to admire them. They had a daddy, a real one who loved them. My heart also ached, longing to know an unconditional love that a good father gives. *Will I ever experience this?*

I began to study faith in a new way, and I was excited because it felt like God was lining things up for me as I walked through this new season in my faith. During the convention, I learned that Dr. Savelle had a Bible School in Crowley, Texas, only 40 minutes from our home in Arlington. I enrolled in August and found myself sitting in Bible School not even 30 days later when the semester started in September. I asked the Lord to be "my daddy" and send me to school and set me up. I wanted to be able to go to school without worrying about bills, to have all of my needs met like a little girl should. I prayed that God would teach me how to be HIS daughter. I didn't truly understand this kind of relationship, nor had I ever experienced it, except for a short season with Dad #4 in Eldorado, Arkansas.

It was an amazing gift from God that I had such a great job. When I called my boss and told him I was going another direction, that I was going to school to pursue something new, I wanted to give him 30 days' notice and offer to train my replacement or do whatever I could to help him fill my position. He said he would get back with me. This was in 1997, when the travel industry had been hit hard and there was hiring-freeze industry wide. I was very successful in my position. I serviced clients, and building relationships is something I did well. My boss got back to me and asked if he eliminated my travel, would I be willing to continue working from home at my current salary. I recognized this as my Heavenly Father making provision for me.

I completed my first year of Bible School without the stress of finding a new job in order to keep up with my bills and the kids' school. Of course, Joel paid child support and always helped take care of the boys. He and their grandfather always made sure the boys had everything they needed, and it was a tremendous blessing.

My first year in school was a year of faith. I went to Israel, Africa, Albania, and the UK many times. I went on all these trips by faith, meaning I didn't have the money to pay tuition, my house payment, bills, and travel expenses on mission trips. But GOD made a way for all of it. I was in Africa for three weeks, and I only had $100 to take with me. If you have ever traveled internationally, you know the layovers alone can make $100 disappear quickly. I was not afraid. I just went, and by the time we arrived, I only had about $50 left for three weeks. Our food was provided, but we had to purchase bottled water. I am not real sure how God stretched that $50, but I came home with change in my pocket. It was a life-changing experience to live with these people in the bush. Translators assisted us during the ministry time. I fell in love with Africa and its people. They taught me how to worship in every circumstance. They walked for miles just to attend our meetings. I came home, changed forever. The school year ended and so did my job. I needed to find a new job and a new place to live because I could no longer afford my mortgage. But my faith was strong.

I leased out my Arlington home. Sean moved in with his father. And Jered and I found a little single wide trailer with a floor that could cave in at any moment. It was only $500 a month, and it was on Eagle Mountain Lake. God is so good. He knew I loved water and we had a beautiful view of the lake and a marina with beautiful cruisers on it. I was amazed. It wasn't a stylish high rise apartment, however the outdoor view was amazing and I was grateful. I made our place look like a model home on the inside. My furnishings didn't fit, but we made the best of our little two bedroom singlewide. I was still without a job. The tenant who was moving out had a boat cleaning business. She cleaned and cared for people's boats during the week for them to enjoy on the weekends. I asked her if she would introduce me to the owners with the idea that I could take over her clients, and she agreed. I began cleaning boats every day. The boys and I often did it together, and it's still is one of my fondest memories. There was no pressure, and I was on the water around wealth and beautiful people who appreciated what I was doing. It provided for all of our needs and the boys and I made memories.

I was so passionate about the call of God on my life, and I was beginning to walk in it. I was mopping my floor at home one morning when I saw myself on a stage ministering to women. It was like a movie reel, and I cried out to the Lord, "YES… that is what I want to do." I cried as I continued mopping the floor. This was a vision, and it was the first time it felt REAL and not just a figment of my imagination. It was time to enroll for the second and final year of Bible School. Suddenly, the hiring freeze in the travel industry had been lifted, and my company offered me a sweet position in Chicago. I loved Chicago. I had been there often since the central US was my territory. I was so torn because I really wanted to attend the second year of Bible School and complete the process I had started.

After much prayer, I went with my heart and began to plan financially for how I could stay in Texas and complete Bible School. Sean was struggling and wanted to continue living with his dad. Joel was remarried by now, and I loved his new wife. She was so good to my boys. Joel and Janet were involved in a mega church in Oklahoma, and Joel was even on the worship team. Again, I wondered if I had given up on our marriage too soon because Joel was living for God now. Maybe I just hadn't been patient enough to walk through that painful season with my children's father. However, I had to move forward with my plan because all of those things were over now. They were in the past. Jared and I found a rental house in Crowley, near the Bible School. It was an old house, but I made it a beautiful home, and Jered and I began to explore our surrounding community in Crowley.

During the break between the first and second year, I worked, moved, and prepared for the semesters ahead of me. The travel company had given me a $500/month car allowance. With that gone, I needed to sell my new Nissan Maxima. It was sporty with all the bells and whistles, and I loved that car. However, when I went to sell it, I could not get what I needed in order to pay it off. I called the bank and told them I could no longer afford the car, that I had tried to sell it, and I asked for their advice. They told me to give it back voluntarily, so that is what I did. And now, I had no vehicle.

Meanwhile, Steve had come back into my life. I had missed him terribly. In retrospect, I am not sure how or who rekindled the relationship, but we were together that summer. He found me a cash car, a little SAAB, and it was adorable. It was a five speed and it was white, one of my favorite colors on a car. It had a sunroof and cool wheels. If I remember correctly, I believe he bought the car for me. I was feeling favor all around me. God worked it out. The car was not new, nor was it as shiny as my last one, however it still had a cool, classic vibe to it. I drove that car with pride. When It would not start, Jered and I would lay our hands on it and command it to start, and it would.

Steve was not in total agreement with me going to a Word of Faith college. He went to CFNI (Christ For the Nations International), another local Bible School which focused on worship at that time, and he was a worshiper. He supported me, but I acknowledged it was difficult because he was raised in a different faith. He had a great family, and they lived in East Texas. He grew up in the Assembly of God denomination his whole life. His mom and dad were still married, and he had the family I always dreamed of having. During this round of our relationship, he proposed to me, and I was going to marry him. I loved Steve. He was my David, a true worshiper, and we had this crazy chemistry I had never experienced. He made me laugh all the time, and I always felt adored and honored with him. I knew he would be faithful to me. Steve was a good man and an excellent father, and he loved me unconditionally. My family loved him, and my boys loved him.

The only issue we had was the differences between the Word of Faith beliefs and the Assembly of God beliefs. This was my perception as I was growing and finding my way in my own faith. My internal fear over the distinctions was huge. I felt accepted and a part of something with the Word of Faith. I finally felt I belonged somewhere and to something that was good. Even though I knew he didn't agree with some aspects of my faith, we worshipped the same and we believed in the same God, and this man adored and supported me.

Still, my fears destroyed our relationship—and once again, we were both left heartbroken.

I hurt him and that hurt me even more. I was trying to follow my passion and what I felt God was calling me to. I just didn't have the maturity or the healing to work through it with him. Looking back, our break up clearly stemmed from ignorance and fear on my part. Had I been further along in my own healing and emotional maturity, it could have turned out differently for us. As it was, I had lived my whole life not belonging anywhere. I lived my life feeling like an orphan, and I finally found faith, and the Word of Faith community helped me. I was terrified to leave it. Still, looking back now I see that I was foolish in the way I handled things and once more, I ran from a good man. A lack of knowledge and immaturity in one's growth process will lead to ignorant decisions.

My second year of Bible School began, and I was on fire to win souls and save the world. I served an internship at First Super Kids at Eagle Mountain Church. Jered, my youngest, was in Super Kids at the time. Watching my seven-year-old son raise his hands in worship and dance to the music melted my heart. Jered is a worshiper, and I dedicated His gift to the Lord during that season.

Chapter Eight

THE POWER OF FORGIVENESS

L IFE REALLY PICKED UP A POSITIVE MOMENTUM FOR ME DURING this season. Then I received a phone call from my mother asking me to pray for Husband #3. He had been diagnosed with a rare cancer and wasn't expected to live much longer. I began sending him healing tapes, and I even called him and prayed for him over the phone and told him that I knew God wanted to heal him. I continued sending him cassette tapes on healing, and he thanked me. A few months later, he was in Athens, Texas for a celebration of something my brother had accomplished. I am not sure if it was his graduation from nursing school or another moment, but Dad #3 got really sick and had a horrible infection that was related to his chemotherapy port. It was life threatening.

Mom called me and asked me to pray because they were not sure he would make it back to San Antonio. I grabbed the boys and drove to East Texas. I stopped to purchase grape juice and crackers, as I felt the Lord wanted me to take communion with him and pray for him. I dropped my boys off at my mom's and went to the hospital. She wanted to join me, but I wanted to go alone. I arrived at the hospital prayed up and expecting God to show up. I felt a strong anointing and knew God was walking in there with me as I felt His presence beside me. As I entered his room and looked into his eyes, the Lord told me that he had not forgiven himself and *that* was what was killing him, not the cancer. I walked over to his bedside and said, "God has forgiven you. I have forgiven you. But you have not forgiven yourself. Let it go today and God will heal you." I prayed, and I can tell you exactly what I said, as it is as clear to me as if it happened yesterday. I prayed, "Father, I ask you to heal this man from all disease and help him forgive himself, as I know you have already forgiven him. Father, I ask you to do this for me. In your precious name I pray. Amen."

God healed him! He lived a healthy life for several years. I was completely and wholly set free as I turned my pain from him into a blessing for him. God healed him. And God healed me. It was the most amazing experience: I forgave him, led him to the Lord, prayed for him to be healed, and God healed him. I was more than amazed at the goodness of God. I left East Texas with my sons and drove back to Fort Worth to continue my school and my life—set free from abuse and shame!

When I returned to school that week, an opportunity to intern for Embracing His Grace became available. It was the second time it had opened up, and I took it. Embracing His Grace was a wonderful ministry that focused on leadership development, led by an amazing woman, Ginger Ziegler. She was a mother figure in my life, and I adored her. She had a vision to take the leadership school into the prison system, so I assisted her with her goal. We ministered in both men's and woman's prisons, and I led ministry in the women's section. Gatesville Prison was a huge facility, and we served many units. Every week, I would take a group of leaders there with me, and we would teach leadership in various units simultaneously, followed by a graduation for the inmates. I relished this season. I had never been in prison, but only by the grace of God. I believe that giving in this capacity set me free from the burdens of my past transgressions and made His grace even more real to me.

I met so many amazing women who were incarcerated. We were doing a large crusade through Mike Barber Ministries, and I was loving on the women before the meeting started when I ran into Darlene. Darlene was one of the teenagers I would get high with on the weekends when I was 12 and my father and stepmother would go to another couple's home and play poker. She was one of their daughters, and here she was now, in prison. When I saw her, we embraced immediately, but we couldn't catch up because there were strict guidelines about getting close to the inmates. My heart broke because I thought, *that could have been me. I could be in here just as easily as she is.* I was very humbled and grateful that God had spared my life. Many times, I was protected by God as I was in meth labs and running with the same people as she was. God's grace covered me, and I was profoundly grateful and simultaneously brokenhearted for her. *It could have been me...* I recalled one time when the police came in and took many people, but they didn't take me. They just asked me to leave. God's grace was protecting me when I didn't even know Him. Seeing Darlene broke me and reminded me how much God had protected me, even before I knew who He was.

Throughout my second year of Bible School, I saw many miracles God either did for me or through me for others. After graduation, I went to work at KCM for a few short months until I learned of a position that opened up at JSMI (Jerry Savelle Ministries International) where I just graduated. I worked under Julie Powers, an instructor at the Bible School, and the Dean's wife. Julie was an amazing mentor, teacher, and writer. She became one of my close friends. I am so honored that the Powers were my mentors and helped mold me into the person I am today. I could share so many stories of how God met me where I was during that season.

There was another instructor who taught faith at JSMI, Pastor Sam. He was known as a solid man of faith. A father of six amazing children, I had always admired him because of the dedicated father he was to his children and the man of honor he was to his wife. He and his wife both taught at the Bible college. She received a cancer diagnosis three years prior (that none of us knew about). She fought the illness in faith and believed in God for healing, until she ultimately crossed over to be with Jesus. I watched her fight the good fight of faith—and she won! My heart broke for their six children who adored their mother, and I found myself praying for their family a lot. Sam and his wife had been married for many years. They grew up together, started a church in Fort Worth, and went on many mission trips to Albania. I admired their faith to go beyond what was believed possible. They just did it, and they worked together as a team in ministry. Their children all served in ministry with them as well, and I loved the family that I saw modeled in front of me.

I saw Pastor Sam at a graduation ceremony for the Bible School, and he looked very lost without his wife. My heart broke for him, as it had only been eight months since she had passed. While I was serving in the green room, where ministers prepare to speak and teach, I invited him out for coffee. I said, "Pastor, I am sure it is so difficult to get on with life and even know what to do next. If you would ever like to get together for coffee with a group of us, please let me know." Then, I asked him what he did for fun in this new season.

He replied, "I fly my kite and plant flowers and work in my yard."

I asked what he did with other people.

"I don't."

I left my invitation on the table.

Another Bible School graduation was complete, and summer was in full force as we prepared for the next group of Bible School students coming in. Several months later, out of nowhere... my phone rang. It was Pastor Sam. He asked me if I would like to have coffee. I said, "Sure," and we set a time and a place. He picked me up and was the most respectful man I think I had ever met. When he opened the car door for me and put me in the car, he came around and sat in the driver's side seat with tears in his eyes. He said, "You are the first female, besides my daughters, who has sat in that seat since my wife passed." My heart melted, and my eyes teared up because of his pure heart. We went for refreshments, because I later learned he didn't like coffee. We talked for hours. He was such an innocent man. He had been a faithful husband, a faithful minister for the Lord, and truly a man of God. He asked me out again, and we went to a church meeting to see Charles Capps. This was a bold step for him because in those circles everyone knew us, and here we were, out together and both single. When that date ended, he walked me to my door and said thank you.

He was either so pure of heart, or just didn't know how to move forward without his late wife—or both. We talked for hours on the phone and continued to discover things about one another. He and I had a true love for the Kingdom of God and saving souls, and we did that well, even though we did it differently. We were truly opposites who had ended up in the same place. After many late night telephone conversations, he asked me out for a third date, and this time he included his children. The girls cooked dinner at his house, as they were all still young and living at home. I think he wanted to see if I would pass the kids' test. I fell in love with all six of them. They were a beautiful family.

Soon thereafter, he asked me to marry him. My first response was, "I think it is too soon since your wife's passing." It had not even been a full year, and I requested to sit down as a family and talk about this decision. I had been single for over 11 years, and I came from a different background than he had. All the kids said they were okay, but my gut instinct was that they needed more time, and we needed more time. However, I ignored those feelings, and I said *yes*. We were married just three months later. Sam was an upstanding man. He didn't even kiss me until just before our wedding day. His pureness of heart was so beautiful to me. I had never met a single man who was that pure and honorable. And coming from the childhood and culture in which I was raised, his mannerisms with me and with his children were truly refreshing.

We married in the heat of August in Texas on the hottest day of the whole month. We had a very small wedding, and then we were off to California for our honeymoon, and soon after that we were on the mission field. We traveled to Albania often, as he had a church planted there. I fell in love with Albania. He merged his Fort Worth church with Dr. Savelle's new church in Crowley. I was a member of The Potters House in Dallas, however my life was changing. Dr. Savelle traveled a lot, and he asked us to pastor the church, and we did it together. I was now a pastor's wife and an associate pastor at Heritage of Faith Christian Center. Pastor Sam did the preaching, and my role was to grow the leadership staff and develop discipleship programs.

I was very happy, and this man treated me better than anyone I had ever met. If we drove separately, he would meet me in the driveway and help me with my things and ask me how my day was. He was a dedicated husband. I never even pumped my own gas or washed my own car. He made sure I always had a full tank of gas and my car was always clean. We were great together.

Life was rocking along, then I received a phone call that Daddy #3 whom God had healed, saved, and forgiven had taken his own life. I was devastated and angry at the same time. I called my mom and told her that if it was okay with my brother and the family, I would be honored to minister his funeral service. I felt like I was still in the fight, but I knew to honor that man out loud and bury him would mean God still won. The thing was, I felt my brother needed it. That was his daddy. Daddy #3 was a good father to my brother, and there was so much to honor him about. I had forgiven him and loved him unconditionally; my heart held nothing but love.

The real healing came to the rest of the family who knew what had happened to me in the past. They watched the broken little girl they knew honor the man, who despite inflicting abuse, had been a real dad to me in so many ways. I focused on the great memories, made people laugh, and watched healing take place in the chapel that day. God is so good! Walk in forgiveness and love and God will restore to you everything the devil and life itself tried to destroy. Fight back with love because love always wins. This lesson on forgiveness has carried me through life. To this day, I forgive often, and I choose not to sweat the stuff that doesn't really matter. If it is in the past, let it stay there and find a way to love the situation. Ask the Lord for wisdom on what you can learn. It will amaze you when His grace and love cover you.

My world was rocked once more at the beautiful age of 40. My husband and I were running so fast doing missions in Albania all while pastoring for Dr. Savelle. I was so happy and felt like I was living the dream. Then things began to shift... I felt it coming. My orphan mentality followed me, even if from a distance. I didn't realize that was happening until much later in life however, though. When I felt change coming, I threw up my invisible defense shield. I made several mistakes as I worked out my new role as a church leader. I had a background in corporate America. I was used to setting goals and getting things done. I didn't understand how to soften my drive in ministry. It is much different working with volunteers. Circumstances changed at the church, my season of leadership in ministry came to an end, and God directed me back into the secular business world.

I became a realtor, and my husband and I planted a new church in Burleson, Texas, not far from where we lived. We were sent out of our position at Dr. Savelle's church with honor and blessings. Our season there lasted a short three years, but it was a beautiful season nonetheless. One of my best friends to this day is Dr. Savelle's daughter, Jerriann. During the transition, she moved back into the area, and she and her husband took the role of pastors at the church. I loved the way Dr. Savelle embraced his children and always promoted their dreams. Jerriann walked in her calling, and this role was just the beginning of what God had for her. Jerriann and I walked through so many seasons together, and we still do today. It amazes me how God will bring people into your life and they become like family. Jerriann was my 3AM friend. If I ever needed to be just be vulnerable and talk, she was always there to listen and pray with me. She never judged me for my shortcomings; she just loved me unconditionally. Her sister Terri was the same way. I am so grateful for these relationships.

Planting a church is not for the faint at heart. My husband had done it several times before and he was a man of faith, so we birthed a church and had our first service within seven days. I was working in real estate to help support us and launch the new church. We didn't have a youth pastor, so shortly after we launched, I took on that role because I love youth. We started with two teenagers and grew to about 50. I was involved in all-city events, such as "See you at the Pole" for prayer, as well as many other community events. I felt this was my mission, and I loved it. We didn't have a youth band, so since my youngest son played the guitar, I asked Jered if he would put together a band for the youth group and lead it.

He responded, "Mom, no one knows how to play in a youth group."

I encouraged, "Teach them—just make it happen."

Jered did a phenomenal job. Eventually, I began to host a Battle of the Bands once a year, and it was a blast. This season of life was one of my favorites. I love young people. Our band might not have been the best, but our vision was about bringing people together and creating community. People need a place to belong, and that is what we created. My fondest memories were created in that season of teenagers. Having 50 youth at my house for a lock-in was one of my favorite events. I didn't see myself as a pastor, rather as a 'mom' to many. With my difficult childhood, I had so much compassion and love to pour into these young people. I still see many of them on social media, and it excites me to see their little families. It makes me proud!

When I got into the hearts of these young people, the stories of their families wrecked me. Two girls whom I adored came into the group. Their mom was in prison. In fact, their whole life, they watched their mom go in and out of prison. My heart embraced them, and I loved them deeply. Teenagers go through so many things in life, and I watched them as they too felt orphaned. I had so much empathy because I knew that feeling and struggled with it as well. I didn't identify what that feeling actually was until much later in my life. But their experiences struck a nerve in my soul. Looking back now from a healthier place in my life, I can see how some of my actions and responses to certain people and events, stemmed from my own hurt, fear of abandonment, and feeling like an orphan. In life, I believe it's easy to slip into auto-pilot and do what we believe is expected of us instead of genuinely being who God created us to be. Learning to live from a place of authenticity takes time to STOP and listen to what God is saying. I finally learned how to listen.

Launching a new church, starting a new business in real estate, and blending two sets of children (especially considering there were eight of them) was challenging. Our children came from two different worlds, so blending was extremely difficult, and it put tremendous stress on our marriage. After nine and a half years of trying, we gave up and divorced. I regret we didn't get help or coaching on how to combine our families.

Ministry, too, can be so difficult. It is hard to show your scars and your weaknesses for fear that you will be judged and lose credibility. My youth and inexperience in ministry and family only complicated our situation. I had never revealed my past to our blended family; it wasn't something my husband wanted me to share. My husband didn't even want to know details. Sam preferred I leave it in the past and move on. I did end up sharing my story with his girls much later in time, but unfortunately, I carried the shame of my past all through the early years of my season in ministry. It was something I felt embarrassed about, a darkness that threatened my capacity to minister to other people. I didn't learn until much later in life how embracing our challenges and struggles can lead to growth and maturity. I am grateful for all the seasons I have weathered now—not just the sunshine—because now I know God will guide me, love me, and direct me if I will call upon Him when life is hard. The choice has always been mine. Sometimes I just didn't want to listen, and that is where I have regret or shame about things that can't be changed. His grace covers those moments as well. I know God forgives me when I ask, just like He does with anyone else who seeks Him.

Even though I worked fulltime at the Bible School, I had never been a pastor's wife or co-pastor of a church. I knew I needed to honor the church family and my husband, so I did it to the best of my ability. We just didn't know how to persevere through the blending of families to meet all eight children where they were in their individual hearts and give proper attention to their old wounds and new expectations. My perceptions were being developed in this season also. I learned that our perceptions can be wrong sometimes because we filter them unwittingly through our wounds. The way we see things can seem so real and right in our own hearts, only to learn later that we could have done it differently. Knowledge is power, but it can be painful, too.

I was not equipped to take our blended family to the next level, to be strong to fight my way through our difficult times. My idyllic expectations of having a large "in love" family who would do life the same as a biological family were unrealistic. My wounds informed my actions, and my desires to belong in a family were so deep. And so, rather than one whole family, I constantly felt like a referee between my kids and his kids. I loved them all. But we somehow failed to stand together and deal with things from a healthy place.

Our children were raised in two different cultures. My boys grew up seeing two parents live very differently after they divorced. My boys saw me and their dad, Joel, work together to be a family the best we could. Joel had remarried a wonderful woman, whom I loved. She loved my boys, and I will forever be grateful for her. Joel and Janet were not in ministry. They lived regular lives, and Joel worked fulltime and still played in bands, both secular and at their local church. I had been in ministry fulltime for several years and was still trying to decipher the "rules" and walk in a more relational approach with others, to just love God and trust it will work out. I didn't like all the rules of religion. I just loved God and never believed you had to do this or that to earn His love. I believed the Bible, and I believed we should do what it instructs. I did my best, although I think my free-spirit was misunderstood at times. The pieces of my shattered life were being reconstructed, and I was learning in ways I didn't even realize.

My husband's kids were raised in church and home-schooled their whole lives. Their frame of reference about family was built at home with limited or no exposure to how other families worked. My husband and I didn't learn to meet in the middle and seek first to understand. And while I admired what they had, I didn't know their family and home structure from personal experience, only from the outside looking in. If I had to do it all over again, I would have insisted we date for a longer season, allowed everyone get to know one another better, and organically blend in friendship and respect.

Instead, I was a Mama Bear, and he was a Daddy Bear, both fighting for our kids. We just didn't figure out how to fight *together* to make it work. In anger, we can say and do stupid things. I can only speak for myself, but personally, I wish we would have handled things differently. I made a lot of mistakes trying to make things happen that were not mine to make happen. I worked hard to make family time and family connection matter. However, I didn't consider how they felt as much as I could have. I had not lost a mother at a young age. I didn't know how to release the difficult things to God and allow Him room to move.

I later came to understand that my mindset for years had been to protect and fight for my boys because no one stood up for me as a child. It was a trigger I didn't even realize I had, but I have learned it since. It was a sad season—for all of us in many ways. For me, my dream that we would be a model ministry team with our blended family was shattered. His kids, whom I still love and respect, are doing well and I am so proud of them, even though I don't see them much anymore. Ten years have since passed, and I am 56 at the time of this writing. We have all since grown and experienced new things.

When we go through seasons laced with difficult life experiences, we must slow down and look for the lessons we need to learn. There is always growth available to us in the lessons. We need to be careful to get over anger. I have said some stupid things in anger. Words are powerful, and they can never be taken back. We must pray that those we have hurt can forgive us, and we must be patient with them as they process their feelings. We may have to work a little harder to earn back broken trust.

Chapter Nine

BECOMING MY OWN WOMAN

A FTER GOING THROUGH A HEART-WRENCHING DIVORCE from Sam, I felt like a total failure. I was doing well in real estate, still, I slipped into a dark place. I felt so alone. I am thankful my Keller Williams family embraced me and kept me pressing toward something greater because for a while I rebelled against all the things I knew. I just let my hair down for a moment and didn't care—and it showed. I was angry because I had fought for my marriage. I communicated over and over, but the heart and head were not connected. So, in my mind, I failed.

I had our dream home, and it was empty. I walked through my home and remembered the precious memories of small groups and relationships. I missed our family gatherings where I cooked for the family, and we swam in our pool with all the grandchildren. Since Sam was ten years older than me, his children were having babies during the final years of our marriage. I fell in love with those grandbabies. My fondest memories were the large family gatherings we hosted. When we were all together, there must have been 25 of us. Summers were amazing, and there was some kind of event every weekend. I loved the family! But it was suddenly gone.

When the divorce became final, my youngest son Jered was away at college, and Sean was working in East Texas. I sat in the dream home we built together, alone. I kept it for about a year, and then the real estate market crashed. There were foreclosures everywhere. Fear gripped me worse than it had in a long time. I placed our dream home on the market and prayed for a good offer.

I didn't have a church home anymore, so I bounced around searching for a place to belong. It is such a vulnerable feeling to be displaced when you leave a place of comfort and security. I was not too worried about making a living because somehow I always did well. I continued working hard and selling real estate. I know God was with me. He never left me. He always provided for my needs. The triggers of shame, failure, isolation, and abandonment all came full circle for me, and they crashed down hard.

I wish I would have talked to a professional about the feelings I didn't understand, but I didn't. I had one amazing close friend named Susan. She was my rock. Susan lived down the road from me, and daily I would stop by, and we would sit out on the porch and talk. To this day, we refer to this season of our lives as our porch ministry. She was going through her own battles with kids and life. She offered me a safe place to just be me and bleed. She spoke life into me, and she is still one of my favorite people. Susan had an understanding about God's love that I didn't. She poured love into my life like no other person had before being in ministry.

She was very Kingdom-minded. Actually, I had not heard that term before, and I didn't understand it. She introduced me to Bethel Ministries and Bill Johnson. I began to be fed and healed under that ministry. Susan was attending a church that I soon began to attend. This church was so different than other churches I had attended. It was so free, and there were no titles. The pastor wore flip flops, and people called him by his first name. The worship was so deep and meaningful. I sat in that church for a year and didn't do anything but heal and soak it all in. I learned in this bleeding season to absorb and allow the Lord to love on me. I learned to sit still.

I still lived recklessly in some ways. I loved to dance, and my little sister and I went dancing often. I just wanted to get lost and not think about the pain. Music and dancing was my escape. God was with me in those moments; I just couldn't wrap my head around what He was doing. My oldest son and I got a tattoo together. I just did whatever I wanted. I now have three tattoos. It is funny to me now because I was 48 years old and getting tattoos. The hippy chic in me was coming to life. I was finding myself again and beginning to love myself again.

I sat on my back porch where I spent a lot of time. It was a beautiful oasis with a palm tree and a beautiful pool. I decorated it like a resort with outdoor curtains and beautiful flowers. It was my secret place with the Lord. It was in this place I asked the Lord if it was possible for me to ever have a true love? A love that was truly one flesh, a person I could do life with— kingdom-life with. I was hungry for a partner that I could just be myself with and love freely. I wanted to experience unconditional love with my husband. I wanted to love wildly and give my heart away to someone who would not waste it. I desired to be with someone who just got me and loved me no matter what. I made a list of what I thought I wanted. The list included: he must be a worshiper; he would love music; preferably he would be tall because I like to wear heels; he would love family; and he would have a servant's heart. I asked that he would be real and authentic, and not religious, but relational. He would be a lover of life and God. He would be confident in his manhood. He would be strong. And I gave my list to God.

In 2011, a loan officer I worked with asked me to help his Pastor find a new home and to sell his current ranch. My loan officer knew I understood ministry and how to be a minister and an agent at the same time. I knew who the man was because of his musical recordings in the past, but I didn't know him personally. I made contact with him, and Pastor Michael set a time to meet at Starbucks in March.

I was a nervous wreck, as I prepared all of the showings and mapped them out in my car because I am directionally challenged. I met Michael and his staff members at the Starbucks, and I was a little taken aback. This man stood at the counter as I walked in—6'4" and full of swagger! He was a beautiful man, and Michael had this way about him that was charming and gorgeous. I had never experienced anything like it, and despite all attempts to fight it, I physically melted inside. I am never nervous at buyer consultations, but this one was different. Chatting at the table at Starbucks, I learned a little more about what he was looking for. There was something different about him. Michael didn't appear to be religious, rather I could tell he had texture. He was a unique man, and he was just gorgeous.

Our first day of looking at several homes was an adventure. We went to eat sushi after the showings, and I learned more about him. He seemed very laid back and just different than anyone I had ever met. He was cool and charismatic. I left that appointment wondering what God had planned for me and—*why am I meeting this man?*

Michael had a small ranch just south of town that he needed to sell. It was a beautiful property, and he had put a lot of money into it. I listed the property, and we continued looking at homes. His home had to sell before he could purchase a new one. There were some unfinished things he was working on in order to sell the property at the best possible price. I was able to assist him with the finish out, and we became great friends in the process. The home turned out beautifully, and we were able to get him top dollar for the market at that time. It took two years to get an offer and close due to complexities with the buyer and the real estate market in general.

Michael and I spent a lot of time together working on his ranch and scouting new properties, and after a year of friendship with him, I found myself falling deeply in love with him. We shared with one another our previous pain in life and relationships. We were both broken people who had suffered in the past and now wanted to focus on the present. I loved that he understood ministry. The ministry he came from was much different than what I had been involved in. I was intrigued to learn about the different cultures of ministry.

He had been married for about 34 years, and he wasn't ready for anything other than friendship. He made that clear. I understood and was very happy to be his friend. He made me laugh. When we would meet people, they were always drawn to us like magnets. I loved how this man could connect with people so easily the way I did, and we did that together often. We shared many meals together, typically sitting at the bar, where we'd end up leading people to the Lord and inviting them to church. We called it our bar ministry. It was so refreshing because it wasn't ministry in a standard church building; rather, we were effectively and naturally reaching people outside the walls of the church. People looked excited when we walked in the door. They became "our people," and we always poured life and positivity into them. This is one part of the man I fell in love with. We were the same brand. We loved people the same way, and I had never experienced this before.

One of his love languages was gifts. As we became best friends, he began giving me Gucci, Christian Louboutin, and many other amazing shoes. He would take me shopping and be my personal shopper, and everything he chose for me was perfect for my curves. He exposed me to a life of gifts like nothing I had ever had before. I had always been more frugal because I had to be. I had been a single mother for so many years, and when I was married before, we poured our money into the church and didn't do much for ourselves in that way. I loved the shoes and clothes he gave me.

He taught me not be ashamed of my curves. I always hid them, because I had learned over time that it's typically considered inappropriate to show them in the church world. So, I dressed very conservatively because of where I had come from. Do you remember the story I shared about receiving looks from the church women about my appearance when I was a new Christian? That insecurity never left me. I dressed cute, but never sexy, and I never wore fitted garments that revealed my curves. But Michael liked my curves. He made me come alive in ways I had buried long ago. He knew my whole story about dancing and the life I came from, and he embraced it. He was impressed with what God was doing and had done for me through the years. I never felt shame from him.

He was the most unique man I had ever met. It wasn't long before I began attending his church. I didn't really get involved until much later. I sat and I observed. Then Michael and I would have a meal almost every week after service. However, I never spoke to him at church because he was very private, and he didn't want people to assume we were dating. He was an amazing teacher of the Word, and

I knew he studied to deliver a message every week, and I respected his time to do that. He was an incredible worshiper as well. Our relationship was sweet and built on a deep friendship.

I fell in love with the people at his church, and they embraced me as "Pastor's Friend." I have never met such loving and giving people as I did at his church. The church was very diverse, and I loved it because I believe that is what heaven looks like—all races coming together as human beings made in God's image. It has nothing to do with the color of our skin. I have always surrounded myself with all races because I think people are people—and people are beautiful. We all bleed the same color, and though it may pulse under different shades of skin, we are all one race—the human race.

During the time our relationship was developing, my dream home from my previous marriage finally sold, and I moved to a town about one hour away. My boys were both home. Jered graduated from college, and Sean moved back home. I was happy to have my boys with me for a short season. We moved to Granbury, Texas and lived there for a year. It was time for the boys to launch into adulthood and move out. When they did, I moved in with a dear friend, and we shared her home, as she had just come out of a bad marriage. Our friendship really deepened, and I now had a group of girlfriends whom I adored. We ladies traveled a lot that year, as we were all healing from breakups. There were five of us who made plans together often. To this day, we are all still close, even though some are married now. Having a tribe of girlfriends was so healing for me. Women need each other, and I truly have the best girlfriends. Elia (the friend I moved in with) and I still travel together often to this day. She is my BFF at Keller Williams. We have many treasured memories.

In 2014, I turned the BIG 5-0, and I wanted to do something amazing. Michael gave me and my two closest childhood friends, Valarie and Tammy, a trip to Cabo San Lucas. He paid for all of us, and this trip I will treasure forever. Tammy, Valarie, and I had been friends since we were 13. Valarie and I were living for the Lord, and Tammy was trying, but had not quite been able to overcome things from the past that we all grew up with. We stayed at the most beautiful resort, which was all-inclusive, so we ate well and had lots of fun.

They were shocked that Michael, who was "just a friend" would pay for all of us to go celebrate my 50th birthday.

We created precious memories on our trip, but it was also during our stay that we noticed Tammy wasn't well. We didn't know what it was, but something was wrong. Valarie and I would get up early and sit on the beach with our Bible to pray, journal, and connect with God. It was amazing to do this with my close friend. The Lord put it on both of our hearts to pray with Tammy and ask her to renew her commitment to God, and we offered to baptize her in the beautiful pool right in the middle of the resort, and she agreed. Tammy floated for what seemed like hours after that. She said she had never felt so much peace in her life. Still, Tammy's symptoms scared Valarie and me, so we called Tammy's husband because she just wasn't well. He met us at the airport and drove her back to Houston. We learned soon after Tammy had a brain tumor that was huge.

Valarie and I went to Houston several times during her treatment to be with her and help her husband take care of her. Her husband, Burt, was amazing. He cared for her and worked fulltime. He stood by her to meet every need, and I honor him for that. It was so hard to believe though because we were all in the range of 50 years of age. Her sickness lasted several months, then our dear friend Tammy died. Valarie and I were with her as she passed, and it was the hardest thing to witness. I laid beside her and told her I loved her and asked her if her soul was good and if she needed anything from me. She said "I have peace, and I am ready for this pain to be over." Tammy died on her 50th birthday. The hardest part was watching this beautiful soul be in so much pain while there was nothing any of us could do but love her and stand with her.

During the same month of April, another close friend, Leah, was killed in a car wreck. I buried two very close friends in the same week. Leah was a shock. We had just been together that afternoon at a business planning meeting, and she was so on fire and happy. She was going to have the best month she ever had in real estate. She was in a great place. Leah taught me about farm and ranch real estate, and we would go to a ranch she leased and ride horses for hours just to get away and relax. We also went on a camping trip I will never forget.

Later, Leah, Bernie (another female friend in real estate), and I started hosting a real estate booth that we still have today at NCHA. I will never forget the first booth though, as we had no furniture. Since I was living nearby in downtown Fort Worth at the time, we spontaneously emptied my living room and made our booth very homey.

Chapter Ten

A BABY CHANGES EVERYTHING

DESPITE THE TRAGEDIES IN MY LIFE, I WAS DOING WELL. AND my boys, both young men now, began doing well on their own. My youngest son, Jered, began working real estate with me, and we had great success. He was good with people, and I loved having him beside me. Sean was working too, and he met a girl. He told me, "Mom, I am helping this girl. She has no place to live, so I am letting her stay with me for a while until she can get on her feet." I asked him to please be careful, as I didn't want him to get into a situation of having a baby so early in life. He assured me that he was just helping her out and not to worry.

Soon after, I learned from Sean that they were expecting my first grandchild. At first, I was so excited, even though I was concerned about the order in which his life-events were unfolding. But nonetheless, a baby was on the way. I didn't have grandbabies of my own yet, however, I had lots of practice with my ex-husband's grandchildren and with Michael's grands. I loved the experiences! I tried to get to know the mother of my unborn grandchild, but it was challenging. She had come from a difficult family life, and I just wasn't sure about her and my son. I told my son, "Either you will lead your family, or this situation will tear you down because you have not taken the time

to include God. However, we have a baby coming, and we will love that baby. I am with you."

On August 5th I became a grandmother. I had dreamed of being in the room to experience it, but I was unable to because of the mother's wishes. The mother wanted it to be a private time just for her and my son, and I understood even though that was not how my family was. My mom and grandmother were at both of my boys' births, but I respected her wishes.

Leading up to the birth, I was in the middle of a project trying to break into HGTV with a Farm and Ranch show. I was so passionate about it. I found a producer and went away to learn about the director and watch one of the productions he was filming. I stayed at a beautiful ranch for a week and watched them produce a show. This show was a Farm to Fork project, a foodie show. I was able to do a photo shoot for my project and meet some amazing people. While I was away, my grandson Brock arrived.

Still there at the ranch, I received a phone call from CPS that my grandson was born with drugs in his system and he could not be left alone with his birth mother. I was devasted. I had not even seen my grandson yet. I called my mom and asked if she could take a week to go there, and then I would go. They lived in San Antonio at the same time Sean had taken a job in the oil field. The birth mother's father had gotten Sean a great position, and he had always wanted to work in the oil field. My mom stayed with Brock until I could get there.

I returned to Dallas and packed a bag to go meet my new grandson, Brock Alexander Harlan. I fell in love with this child from the start. He was perfect. Jered came as well, and we had a great family time. It is a beautiful memory I treasure of all of us being together. Family is very important to me, and knowing that my boys are with me made me strong. My boys and I are close and have always stuck together. Our family is just that way. My grandparents were that way, and I knew nothing different. Families take care of each other. Even though my history with stepfathers is not positive, I still knew my grandparents' love in my core. They had always believed in me, despite what they knew about my lifestyle. I pray they didn't know everything. They were solid. Becoming a grandmother changed me. I felt a mantel was placed on me from my grandmothers.

A couple of weeks came and went, and it was time for me to leave the baby and return home. After that, I got Brock frequently for long weekends and sometimes weeks at a time. When he was six months old, my son left Brock's mother and came to my house and said, "Mom, I made a mistake, and I need to leave her." I told him we would get through it. I hired an attorney and attempted to adopt Brock. My hope was to get custody for my son, and I could help him raise his baby. As the process was going, just days before our court date, emotions ran high, and Sean decided to go back to her and take Brock with him.

I continued to pray over my "little man," and I got him every chance I could. It was easy when he was an infant because I could take him to work with me. He did many real estate deals with his 'KiKi', the grandmother name I gave myself. As the weeks progressed, I had Brock frequently for weekends or longer, and I sensed something was not right. When I would meet his mom to return him to her, Brock would cling to me, not wanting to leave. I left, crying my eyes out every time because I didn't know what this baby was going through. I expected she was still using drugs and Brock was not being well cared for.

By this time, Michael and I were very close. He was incredibly supportive and loved Brock. We dedicated him to the Lord, and it was precious. I know he loved Brock because he loved all babies. But he stated to me, "Girl, I hope you don't get stuck raising that baby. I couldn't do that at this age." I agreed with him, and I prayed that wouldn't happen. We both saw it was a possibility, and we both feared it could become a reality.

Five years into my relationship with Michael, I believed it was more than friendship because of the way we interacted. We talked or texted daily and saw each other almost every day. There was never a defining moment that we were officially dating, which was at his request. He said, "I can't date because of what I do." Since we weren't "dating," he dated other women, and I dated other men, but somehow we always ended up sharing a meal and talking about our experiences. I questioned him on where he saw us going, and he said, "If I ever get a word from God, I will move forward, but that has not happened." It was a little confusing to me because we acted like we were dating, but he was resolute that in his eyes we were not. When I asked the Lord what this was about, He told me to be a safe place for this man, so I was.

Five years in, I was his best friend with no commitment of anything more ever happening between us. But on the outside, people

who saw us together assumed we were dating. I saw the wounded boy in him. I knew he had been hurt in ministry, lost a son at age 17 in a car accident, and then suffered a divorce years later. He carried a lot of pain, and my heart couldn't leave him. My closest friends asked me if I was alright with the way our relationship was, and I assured them that I was. We were best friends, and I would rather be his friend than be without him. That was truly how I felt.

I noticed that every time we would get close, he would pull away and go out with a new girl—a new friend he had met. And I would be crushed. I rebelled in anger at one point and went out with two different men, but I felt horrible because I knew I was in love with this man. I have never cheated on anyone before, but even without a commitment, I felt like I was cheating on him. Frankly, I was confused most of the time. However, I knew my heart was in love with a man who also felt like my best friend, so for my own peace of mind, I should not go out with another man.

At times he said to me, "I don't know if I will ever marry again." He told me about a long lost love he had many years ago. He wanted to find her. He did, but she lived across the country. They began talking long distance, and I grew frustrated. I knew he was doing what he needed to do, but I began to believe he should let me go and figure things out. At one point, I told him to go to her and figure things out. I knew if he didn't, he would always wonder "what if…" I encouraged him to go, even though I felt gut-wrenching pain as the words left my mouth. After he was set for his trip, she called to cancel because she was in a relationship and feared their visit might jeopardize it. I was relieved. I asked the Lord to shut the door if he was not to walk through it, and God shut the door. I went away with some girlfriends, which I did often.

While I was on the trip, I sat with the Lord and asked to be released from my relationship with Michael. I knew the Lord had asked me to be a safe place for him. I cried alone and decided to end it in my heart. I changed his name in my phone from "Michael" to "JUST SAY NO." When I landed back at DFW, a text popped up from JUST SAY NO. With knots in my stomach, I ignored it. He kept calling, asking to get together for dinner. I told him I was tired and had a full week. He continued to call, and I continued to make excuses for a couple of weeks. I know he felt the distance I was creating, but we had not spoken in person, and I wasn't quite ready. I was working up my courage, but I honestly didn't want to let go. I loved being his best friend, but I knew I had to let it go. My heart was getting hurt over and over. I know it wasn't his intention to hurt me, but my expectations and his were not the same.

He continued to be clear that he had not received a word from God to move forward with us. But from the outside, it felt like he wanted to explore every possibility with other women before deciding whether he wanted me, and he wanted me to be there for him in the process. That was my perception. I am not saying he was doing that, but after five years, it felt that way. I also knew he had been married for 34 years and had only been divorced for five. I knew he needed time to find himself. He and his ex-wife were good friends, and the family still did things together on special occasions, birthdays, etc. I was always included, and I embraced her and his children and grandchildren. I adored his daughter. She was beautiful and he, of course, adored her as well. Being so involved as his best friend, I just didn't know if I wanted to keep being that friend waiting in the wings, and not feeling I was important enough for him to call this what it really was.

I continued to fill my life with as much as I could. Business felt productive. I would get Brock every chance I could, and I loved being his Kiki. This little guy changed my life. He was so adorable, and he was my flesh and blood. He looked just like his daddy when he was a baby. My life was maturing into a new phase. Meanwhile, I had a huge debt to the IRS that was haunting me. I had been paying on this debt since 2011, and every year the new tax would hit me for the current year, so the amount only continued to grow. It didn't seem that my payments were making any impact toward resolving the debt. I spoke to an attorney about what I could do to stop the late fees and catch my breath, so I could pay the IRS actual taxes I owed. After exploring my options, I decided to file bankruptcy—and shame hit me again, hard. I thought, *Here I am, a Christian, a minister of the Gospel, and I am filing bankruptcy.* It was the only decision I felt I could make at the time. I filed Chapter 11 and my payments were a huge $2,100 a month, which was difficult some months to make.

Some difficult events were transpiring at Michael's church. I didn't really understand everything, but I knew it was all attacks. Because he was under so much pressure, I could not bring myself to break it off, so I procrastinated and soon just fell back into the pattern of being his best friend. One day he called me and asked me to come to his house later that afternoon. He had noticed we were not hanging out as much. I was trying to detach my heart. He said he needed to share something with me, and he wanted us to plant flowers as it was April and we did this together every change of season. I had dinner plans with a friend of mine, Jackie, but I called her to reschedule.

I went home to change into my work-in-the-yard clothes, and I arrived at his home, heavy. He seemed different to me, chipper and excited. Glowing, in fact. He said, "Let's go to Lowes, and I have something to share with you." We jumped into his truck and took off. He soon pulled over on the side of the road and said he had received a word from a pastor. I replied, "That's cool," thinking it was about some of the attacks that had gone on at the church. He read the word, or prophecy, that he received and it was right on regarding the turmoil at the church. Then, at the end, he read something like, "This friend you have been with was sent to you by Me. She will be an be an asset to you." I don't have a copy of the prophecy to quote it, but paraphrased, it was close to that. He then continued on to the store for flowers.

I had tears rolling down my face. I was in shock because I had decided just weeks before that I was done with the relationship. He was happy because he had spoken to several people who were close to him, and they had all said, "That is KIMBERLY!" But he saw my tears. He asked me, "What's wrong? I told you when I got a word, I would be all in."

We pulled into Lowes and got out of the truck, and he grabbed me and kissed me like he was in love with me. My head was spinning. I didn't have words. I felt like my life was reeling. He asked again, "What is wrong?"

I answered, "Nothing, I just need to process this." We went on and purchased flowers, took them to his home, and planted them.

I left with so much anxiety in my heart. I was in shock and a little confused with all that was happening. But after several weeks of letting it all settle in, I began to get excited. He was planning everything to move forward in our relationship. On my birthday, he invited all of our closest friends to dinner and surprised me. I thought it was a birthday party, but it was an engagement party. He proposed to me! He had invited special friends and key church members and staff, and they all celebrated with us. He took care of every sweet detail. He knew how I loved bucket filling. (Bucket filling is when you tell people what you love and appreciate about them. The energy from edification of sweet words and how people see you is soothing to the soul.) People were there who I had known for a long time, like my friends Susan and Cindy, plus my close friend Miquette who is my broker at Keller Williams. Miquette has been through every season with me in real estate, and I will forever consider her more as a sister than just a business partner. She has held me together many, many times. The words they showered me with made me cry. Then he started to speak…

He said, "Kimberly thought this was a birthday party, but it is actually our engagement party." He showered me with words, saying he had found his 'good thing' and that I have been his best friend for the last five years. He was grateful for the gift God had given him. He said that God had given Him a word! He got down on one knee, asked me to marry him, then placed a ring on my finger. We set a date just two months away for September 2nd. He announced it to the church and the planning was set in motion. He actually did all of the planning, and we married at a good friend's ranch. It was just beautiful—one of the best days of my life. We took a three-week road trip and started our new life together.

We held a reception later for our children and my mom and dad. They were all excited. My new husband took my oldest son on the patio and said, "Son, I love your mother, and I love Brock. However we are not going to raise your son." Sean said, "Yes sir, I don't expect you to." He made it clear that no one wants to start over at our age. We didn't know what the future held for us.

Not long after, he wanted to sell the home where we lived. I wanted to wait a couple of years to get settled in and get used to being married. Our mortgage was affordable, and the home was beautiful, but he didn't like the city we lived in, so we put it on the market, and it sold the first day. We purchased a home just southwest of there. We found a property that was near foreclosure and was not even on the market. It was still more than we should have purchased because of the amount of work required, but we did it in faith and made a beautiful home on almost 10 acres in a gated community. We lived in our pool house while we remodeled the main home. It was a small 400 square feet bedroom separate from the main house.

Shortly after moving into the home, my youngest son, Jered, ventured out to try something different. He really didn't have a passion for real estate, so he moved to San Antonio with his brother to explore a job in the oil field. That market began to shift, and after three months in San Antonio, he moved back. Since we were now in our main house, I asked my husband if Jered could stay in the pool house a couple of months while he found a new job. Jered had used all of his savings to move to San Antonio and take classes for his new job. Prior to his move, he had given up his apartment here where he had lived for four years. I was proud of him for taking a risk and trying something new. My husband agreed. I reminded Jered that we were newlyweds and asked him to respect our privacy, and he did. He was searching and found a local band. He wanted to try to make it in music by touring. He stayed with us a few months, then found himself a place in Arlington. Today, he has a business of his own, and a band, and he is doing well.

My husband and I worked on growing the church. I assisted him with new members and did what I could to contribute. There was a new real estate company that had shiny toys and seemed to be the up and coming thing in real estate. After being with Keller Williams for 13 years, I decided to leave and go to this new company where every-thing was done online—no brick and mortar. Everyone worked from home. I knew our market was changing rapidly. It sounded exciting, and I tried it. After four months, I knew I had made a mistake. I talked to my husband, and we agreed that I needed to go back to Keller Williams. He had even called my broker and asked her to call me because he saw that I was unhappy. Soon I was back home with Keller Williams and very happy to be back to what I knew.

We experienced a financial attack. He came home from work one day and said he needed to give one half of his salary back to the church in order to accomplish some things that needed to be done there. I responded in support, "God is faithful. We will make it. If that is what is needed, I agree," even though I knew it would put some pressure on me to make up the difference. God is faithful!

However, the stress and pressure quickly intensified for me. I felt I was trying to keep it all together, I allowed the stress to get to me, even though I was fighting it. I put on a little weight because I was overworking and not taking care of myself. But God was faithful to meet our needs. It wasn't always what we expected, but He was faithful.

Chapter Eleven

FULL CIRCLE

As I revealed, I danced in a club when I was approaching 20 years of age. Would you believe God presented me with an opportunity to minister to women in a club? A lady I had just met ran a ministry called Velvet Hearts. They would go into topless clubs and love on the girls with gifts like lip gloss and scented lotions. The day had come when I had committed to go volunteer and minister. On this particular day, I did not feel like going. I had had a long day, and was utterly exhausted. But I had made a commitment, so I stood by it. I was a little nervous about going back into the place God had delivered me from. The minute I walked into the club, I didn't feel anything but a strong purpose for that night. We walked through the club, all the way back to the dressing room. We mingled with the girls and gave them the gifts we brought. There was a girl standing at the stage getting ready to do her set. Her name was Carri Jo. I was drawn to her. I hugged her and introduced myself to her. She didn't have the right shoes, and I sensed that she had never done this before. Carri Jo didn't belong here. I waited for her to come off stage, and when she returned to me, her eyes were filled with tears. They didn't hire her, and she was crying because she was at a desperate place in life in which she really needed the work.

I grabbed her and began to pour out a mother's love to her. She shared her struggle and why she was there. Compassion flooded my heart because I saw myself in her. I was a boy mom, and this girl was so beautiful and could pass for my daughter because we looked alike, and I just felt an immediate love for her. As she cried, I held her and asked her if I could walk her to her car, and she agreed. As we walked out of the club, my spirit was stirring because I knew I was at a divine appointment. I gave Carri Jo my personal cell phone number and asked her to call me. We went to the next club and repeated what we were there to do. The entire night, I couldn't stop thinking about this girl, Carri Jo. I prayed she would call me and regretted I hadn't gotten her number. I returned home with that girl heavy on my heart. I prayed for her, and the Lord showed me I had an appointment with destiny that night, but I didn't understand what that meant.

I received the call I prayed I would get. Carri Jo and I met and the relationship blossomed. She shared her story with me of how she lost her mom at a very young age and she and her twin sister had to figure life out on their own. We continued seeing each other, and I adopted her into my family. Aaron, her boyfriend and the father of her daughter Anna, came to our church, and God moved in their lives. Aaron surrendered his life to the Lord. Later we baptized him in our pool, and not long after that Aaron's brother was saved, and we baptized him.

I had no idea how saying *yes* to serve at Velvet Hearts would change my life forever. We don't always know what God will do in our lives just by being obedient to what He prompts us to do. Carri Jo and Aaron wanted to get married, and I was invited to play the role of mom to her. We created a beautiful wedding for them. It was a moment in life that a simple "Yes, Lord" turned into a huge blessing. Today, Carri Jo and Aaron are my family. They come to all our family gatherings, and I truly love her as my own daughter. Her husband Aaron is amazing as well. When they come to my home, he always asks, "Mom, what can I do to help you?" Aaron is so talented, he can build anything. I always have a list of little things I need help with like hanging lights or shades on my patio, and Aaron makes it happen.

I was so grateful that my husband had a way of ministering to young men. He helped Aaron come alive. I never imagined my experience as a dancer would lend me an opportunity to connect with someone and help them. Had I not lived out that season in my life, I would have never met Carri Jo. Regardless of the painful story of a past I was once ashamed of, I was transparent with my story, naked, and God used it to touch someone else. Carri Jo knew I was not a religious nut. She saw I was a real woman with a past just like hers, and she admired what God had done in my life.

I love walking through life with Carri Jo and Aaron. She is truly the daughter I never had, and I am now one of the mother-figures God has brought into her life. Carri Jo lost her mom when she was in the third grade and prayed for a mother her entire life. God not only brought me into her life, but several other women who said *yes* to being a mom to her. It is amazing how God establishes relationships. My boys also love them and see them as family as well.

As Michael and I approached our second anniversary, a client and friend hosted an event in Rancho Murieta, California for cutting horses, something we both loved. My friend, Leah, had introduced me to the cutting horse sport, and I have I found it to be my favorite. The El Rancho Futurity began in September, so we went to California and had a wonderful time. The owner of the facility, Carol, runs an amazing event at an elegant California setting.

Before we headed to California, we stopped in Atlanta, GA for the celebration of a dear friend of my husband who was walking into a new dream; he was taking over a church. We celebrated with Mo and his wife. It was a precious time. Then, we were California bound. I knew my husband would love traveling to this event. Plus, we needed the getaway. Life was getting a little stressful as I was trying to rebuild my business, pay the IRS, and get on track with our financial goals. When Carol invited us to come, she also asked my husband to hold a church service while we were there.

When we arrived in California, we dreamed and talked about plans for our future. We needed a reset on this trip. Most people don't understand the pressure that pastors go through. They are always caring for the needs of other people, and they want to. But when they are going through pressure and difficulties of their own, they can't share it openly. Rather, they have to keep on course, balance it all, and carry whatever God gives them. The pressure can drain a person, which can then take its toll on a marriage. It takes grit to keep a marriage strong and keep your covenant bulletproof because the enemy will come to destroy it, you and your spouse if you don't guard your life and stand together. Pastoring is something I love, but it comes at a great price. A pastor and his spouse must be nimble and selfless and gracious with one another.

Among our conversations about our future, we also talked about how we could simplify our life. He saw the amount of pressure I was under to rebuild my business, as well as support him and the work needed at the church. He wrote beautiful sentiments about our time. I still have those and treasure them today. He was so good about living out loud and generously shared about our love. We were open about how we felt. Every day in September, he posted about our dates for the month, as it was our anniversary month. Everyone knew we were crazy about each other. Many of my single friends wanted a marriage like ours—not that we were free of stress or issues. We were like any other couple, but we had the foundation of being best friends that carried us through most difficulties. We were still newlyweds though and trying to learn each other's ways. I was trying to learn how to be a Pastor's wife to him, work fulltime, and support my husband's needs. It was a lot! I don't advise any newly married couple to carry all of that at once unless you plan well, live small, and are disciplined to budget and communicate openly.

I don't think women were made to carry such a financial load. I'm not saying women shouldn't work or be involved in the marital finances, but I feel we could have lived a smaller lifestyle, especially since my income was based on straight commission. Some months were amazing in real estate, and some were not so much. Young married couples need to become one and walk through life together, and it takes time to become one. It takes vulnerability and transparency. I don't know that he and I had enough time as husband and wife to walk through the attacks that would soon come. Even though we had a close friendship, we had only been married for two years and had no real issues except for financial challenges. This is my perception anyway.

We arrived back home from our trip on September 17 and our lives fell back into a routine. I was working on a couple of deals that fell apart and caused some additional financial pressure, but we always seemed to make it. While we were in California, we talked about building a barn-dominium on the family ranch I owned in East Texas. My brother and I inherited the small ranch of 40 acres that my grandparents had purchased when I was a baby. My husband and I wanted a place where we could escape and refuel. Our goal was to simplify our life so we could plan for retirement and possibly even put our current home on the market again.

We were financially stretched, and neither of us did well with scarcity. No one likes that. Neither one of us was used to that, and it was draining us both, and therefore our marriage. We put our home on the market briefly, then decided to stay after all. Looking back, we should have left it on the market, but I started making money again and getting my groove back with Keller Williams. Selling a home after living there less than a year presented more financial burdens, so in my professional opinion, I believed we needed to stay past the two year mark. Besides, we loved our home. It really was too much to keep up with because we had to hire help to manage it. So, it continued to drain us financially.

Chapter Twelve

THE BOTTOM DROPS OUT

J UST TWO WEEKS AFTER RETURNING FROM OUR BLISSFUL September anniversary month, I learned that CPS (Child Protective Services) was looking for my grandson Brock. This is what I had feared would happen. His mother was running. She had left the San Antonio area with Brock, and CPS was trying to find him. He was only three years old. My heart raced with panic and fear. Soon Brock's mom called crying and frantically screaming at me to please come get Brock before CPS took him. I was at the office when I took her call. I dropped everything and left to find them. I didn't call my husband first; I just ran to my grandchild who needed me. The whole way to find Brock, I was thinking of the promise I had made to my husband that we would never raise my grandchild, and my emotions raced.

When I finally reached Brittany, I saw Brock, and he looked horrible! I grabbed him and held him and cried. He had been given Zanax, which was why CPS was called. I looked into his eyes, which were glazed over with fear. I will never forget that day. I was standing in a parking lot terrified for my grandson. He needed me and taking him was the only way to keep him from going into foster care. He was wearing a diaper, t-shirt, and flip flops and holding a sippy cup.

His mom had a turquoise bucket of toys and the rest of his things were thrown in a box. My grandson's whole world was in the back of my SUV. The flashback of my own experience as a child, feeling like an orphan, then confronting my life at the Pathways Program came flashing back to me. My only grandson looked like an orphan. I couldn't wait to get him home and bathe him and put fresh clothes on him and hold him safe.

As I was driving back to our home, I dreaded the call to my husband, but I had to tell him what was going on. I told him what had happened and that I was on my way home with Brock. I was knotted up nearly to the point of nausea. I walked in the door, we talked about what had happened, and we both loved on Brock. We were both concerned because we could see he still had drugs in his system. I stayed close to him that week, even sleeping close by in our guest room. I was so fearful the damage would be permanent, I felt the need to be physically near to him. I saw the fear in his innocent little eyes, and my heart broke into a million pieces. *How can this be happening to my only grandson? And to us?* The look in my grandson's eyes was too familiar. It mirrored my pain as a child, and my triggers were firing at full force.

I called my son working in the oil field in San Antonio and told him I had Brock and didn't know what to do. My world was spinning out of control. Sean said, "Mom, God is faithful. I will start looking for a job in the Fort Worth area." Sean worked for Brittany's dad, and that situation wasn't going to last with the hell he and Brittany were going through. Sean soon moved back to Fort Worth and began looking for work. He was not in a place to handle Brock's needs, but having him near to assist me was comforting. This was *his* son, and I wanted him to take responsibility for him. Raising my grandson was not my job. I was Kiki, and I liked it that way. BUT—sometimes you have to put your desires aside and deal with what is in front of you and trust God to work out the details.

CPS called me and wanted to come to our home. I gave them the address and we waited. They looked at our home, made sure Brock was well cared for, took some photos, and left. I had never dealt with CPS before, and all the red tape I had to go through to even take him to the doctor to get checked out was ridiculous. I felt desperate and alone. I was trying to take care of Brock, deal with the challenges of the CPS system, and carry my fears of losing my husband. I had made a promise to him that I would not do this.

Two weeks later, we celebrated the 19th anniversary of the church, which was always a momentous occasion. We had so much going on, the days passed in a blur. The month of October is Pastors Appreciation Month, a time I always looked forward to, but this time, I had no energy to give. For Pastors Appreciation, the church always works with me to do something special for my husband. That year, I was not as involved because my plate was full with Brock and work. I was trying to manage everything and trying to hear what God was telling me.

The staff gave my husband a trip away by himself. In addition, he already had another ministry trip planned. I was hoping to go with him on one of them. I didn't have opportunity to travel with him that much since I worked full time, and we didn't have the resources to travel without my income. The ministry trip was near Galveston, one of my husband's favorite getaway destinations. The staff gave him a week in Galveston, so both trips combined back-to-back, he would be gone two weeks. Even though I knew we needed a break. I also knew *we* needed to go away alone. A lot of difficult events had hit us in a very short time since our return from California.

I was hurt. I wasn't asked how I felt about it or even included in the conversation. I thought I should have been asked if I wanted to go with him. I look back now and I don't know... perhaps he wanted to go away alone, and he might have even asked for that. I will never know the answer. I do know that when I asked the staff why they hadn't shared it with me, I was told, "That is between you and your husband." It was an awkward conversation. I was his wife, and I served beside him, so why wasn't I included?

All of my abandonment fears from the past resurfaced like a tidal wave on top of the orphan-triggers I was having in response to Brock's situation. I was feeling it for Brock and me both. Instinctively, I also felt as if something was seriously wrong the whole time my husband was gone. The trigger of abandonment was vicious in my life, and I didn't even understand it at the time.

I was trying to find childcare for Brock and doctors who could help him. I didn't understand what I was dealing with, and I desperately needed help and guidance. The fear and insecurity I felt during these weeks was more than I could handle alone, but I pressed on to get help and learn what I was dealing with. The reality was that my grandson wasn't a happy, normal three-year-old. He was abandoned, his little life was out of control, and he suffered something beyond my experience. It was the worst attack I can ever remember going through.

When Michael returned home, he attempted to find solutions. He had a family member in Houston who was in ministry, and he reached out to them. They had a beautiful family who wanted to adopt Brock. This family was in my husband's sister's church. They had done foster care for special needs children for years, and it was their ministry. Their daughter, who was married, wanted to adopt Brock because she couldn't have children of her own.

Even though it sounded good, it was too much too soon for me to deal with. Besides, it really wasn't my decision to make—*it was my son's.* Brock is my grandson, and I wanted to make the right decision for his life. I just could not commit to the plan that was presented. I did not feel peace, and it was all happening too fast for me to process. I was trying to keep my promise to my husband, but I could never get to a place of peace. I was between a rock and a hard place.

Meanwhile, I was working on options for Brock as well. My best friend Valarie and her husband offered to help. Since Brock was only three, she said that she and her husband could keep him as long as I needed. I needed time and a good solution for everyone involved. Valarie and Danny are the same age as me, and their offer to help relieved me. My husband was not a fan of the idea, but I knew Brock would be safe, and I would not lose him as my grandson. We met with an attorney and learned that having Brock cross the state line to Valarie and Danny's residence could be difficult and very expensive. Valarie was a court reporter, and she knew that the laws in her state were a little different from those in Texas.

I knew I had to do something. It was so important to me to not lose my grandson. Honestly, I felt angry that my husband would push his feelings about it so hard and fast on me. I expected him to say, "Baby, we will figure this out," but his plan didn't bring peace to my heart. Even though he made it clear where he stood, I didn't feel his plan was God's plan for Brock. And I didn't have a plan yet. A family member told me "this will destroy your marriage" because we were not in agreement on a solution for Brock. Even though I did agree not to raise him before we were married, I could not keep my word. Brock was my flesh and blood. He was the apple of my eye, and I adored him. I could not keep my word to my husband and give up Brock when he needed me most.

We were coming up on Christmas, and Brock had been with us for six weeks. I worked on pulling together a getaway trip for just the two of us, leaving Christmas Day and spending a week away together alone. The church office closes that week every year anyway, and my business is typically slow the week after Christmas, so I planned to take that week off. It would be our time alone and Michael's birthday week. It was the perfect time every year for us to go away together—and this year more than ever. He seemed excited about it, too.

So, I made arrangements for my sons and grandson to go to my mom's ranch in East Texas and have Christmas at Grandma's house. Michael and I would go to a beach house in Texas that a client offered us at no charge. We needed to be alone to reconnect and talk without distractions. Nothing was more important to me. I still felt the disconnect from his trip to Galveston. When he left for that trip, it was a tipping point in which I feared my marriage was in serious trouble. I had so many emotions screaming at me, including rejection. Being the Pastor's wife, I had to put on a happy face, but I failed miserably. It was hard for me to fake anything when there was so much turmoil keeping me overwhelmed. The fates of my relationships with the two most precious people in my life were at stake, and it seemed all the roads ran together. I could not see anything clearly.

Our situation was such a nightmare for both of us. We were still newlyweds, and this was dropped on us as we were already feeling financial pressure from all sides. On Wednesday, December 19, I had not gone to church because I had to do my CE classes for real estate by the end of the year, and I was behind. If not completed by the 31st,

I would not be allowed to stay in business. My husband didn't come home after church.

I texted him to ask if he wanted me to make something for dinner, as we normally went out after church. It was late and he should have been home. There was no reply for about an hour, and I grew concerned. I thought maybe he was out with people. A few minutes later, he called me and asked me if I was sitting down. I asked, "Is everything okay?" I thought something must have happened at church. The sound in his voice told me something was wrong. I asked, "What is it, baby?"

He said, "I am going to read you a letter. This isn't up for discussion or negotiation—just listen." He read me a letter saying he wanted a divorce. That sentence is the only thing I remember. I was in shock. Speechless, I sat down on the bed. I was so stunned, I couldn't even cry. This was my best friend, but this was not him talking to me.

Our little getaway didn't happen. From December 19th to December 25th I was numb. I texting him constantly to please talk to me. I told a couple of people who were very close to me what was going on. I sat home alone on Christmas Eve and cried my eyes out all day. Surely this was all some terrible nightmare I would wake up from—but it was all real. I texted him on Christmas Eve, begging him to talk to me, but he remained silent.

The abandonment, confusion, and brokenness hit me hard. There was a song I must have replayed a million times, "Beautifully Broken". I only remember some of the lyrics, "Here I am Lord, beautifully broken." I sat outside on our patio the entire day, just numb—the same patio where we danced together and watched the wildlife with our morning coffee so many times. It had been our happy place.

Brock was with his father, and they were headed to the family farm. As far as my family knew, Michael and I were getting ready for our trip. Everyone was safe with their families, and I was not going to tell them what had happened and disrupt Christmas for my mom who was not well. She was so happy to have her kids and grandkids home for Christmas that I just couldn't do that to her. I called Jerriann and shared what was going on. She was one of my closest friends, and I cried out my heart to her and told her we were supposed to be leaving tomorrow to go the beach. She was in shock as well because she was one of my friends who admired the relationship my husband and I had. She wanted a love like ours. She asked if I wanted to go to the beach house and offered to go with me after she had Christmas with her parents. She even invited me to have Christmas with them, but I didn't want to be around anyone because all I could do was cry. I told her yes, I would go to the beach.

Jerriann and I left Christmas Day and drove to the beautiful beach house I had reserved for my husband and me. I cried the whole way. Jerriann prayed with me while I sat there numb and speechless. I was grieving almost as if my husband had died. It was the worst feeling I had ever experienced. I have had many heartbreaks in my life, but in these moments, I didn't see how I could ever get past this. Jerriann held me together as we walked the beach and cried, and prayed, and talked freely.

Once we returned home, I texted a counselor-friend, Bob Hamp. I asked if I could get on his calendar after the holidays. I really needed help. He called me immediately after receiving my text. I told Bob what had transpired, and I began sessions with him that week. I knew I needed help. I had lost all control over my life it seemed. I needed to know how to fight this battle because for the first time in my life, I just wanted to die. I was broken. I knew I needed support to stay grounded while navigating these layers upon layers of trouble. My grandson needed me to be strong, and I didn't even know where to begin to walk through this. I saw Bob every week. Counseling helped me think differently and gave me strength for each day. I began to learn about myself and find the girl I had lost once more. Never be too proud to get professional help. The time I invested with Bob helped equip me for the battle I was already in. I prayed to God for wisdom, and Bob helped me identify and absorb the wisdom God was revealing to me, yet through my pain, I had not understood. I will forever be grateful to Bob Hamp. He helped me hold it together, and he walked me through a difficult journey of abandonment and rediscovery.

Brock was scheduled to have surgery on Jan 7 to have his tonsils removed. He was sick often and his tonsils were overgrown. The doctor wanted to do it immediately. A lady from our church who had the kindest heart went with me and was such a precious soul to help me through Brock's recovery so I could work. She also helped me when Brock had to be home for two weeks before returning to daycare.

I was angry and hurt during this season. I continued my sessions with Bob. I battled with questions like: *Who does that to someone who is their best friend?* And *why didn't he just talk to me and share with me if he was unhappy?* I wondered, *was everything he posted all the time on social media about how happy and in love he was just a lie?* My anger had swelled, and it took me a hot minute to get past it. I had such a hard time letting go of *my* perception of our marriage to even try to see it through another lens. *Did I create a false perception about my life? Was it only my perception?*

I was an emotional wreck trying to get my grip on life, meanwhile the Lord provided some comfort and relief regarding the care of my grandson. A sweet friend, who used to lead worship at a church where I co-pastored with Sam years ago, called me. Jered was the lead guitarist on her worship team now, and she asked him out of the blue one day, "How is your mom? I have had her on my heart for days." She asked Jered if she could call me, and she did. When Erica and I spoke, I shared with her what had transpired. She knew a lot because I posted so many photos of Brock and me on social media. She asked if she could help, and we worked out a temporary plan because I didn't know what the future held for any of us. After Brock's surgery, he went to live with Erica while I dealt with the mess I was standing in.

I listed our home, and I lived there until March. My husband and I saw each other often during this time. I had hope that we would work things out. He never specifically gave me hope for that, but we interacted as if nothing had ever happened to us. Brock stayed with Erica for six months, and I saw him every week and took him to his doctor appointments. We were trying this arrangement on a trial basis to see if God was directing her to possibly adopt him, as she had adopted a son who was 14 at this point, and we wondered if this would be a fit. I was not able to hire an attorney, as I was going through a divorce and looking for a place to live. I moved out of our house, but still saw my husband through April. He brought me a beautiful basket filled with goodies for my temporary housing at a ranch on Fletcher Road.

Another time, I had a terrible cold, and he brought medication over to me. I just couldn't believe he and I were going through a divorce.

I wanted to shield Brock from my pain, and I didn't want him to see me in my brokenness. Erica was a life saver and exactly what Brock needed during that time. In April, he came back to live we me. I was staying in the guest house at a dear friend's ranch while I tried to get myself together financially. She allowed me to stay there five months, and I needed that safe place to regroup.

This season was so incredibly heartbreaking and so beautiful at the same time. Being at the ranch was a haven for me. Carol allowed me to live on her beautiful property rent-free so I could heal and get my feet back under me. Brock discovered a love for horses, and I finally got him potty-trained. Country and trees work magic with boys. He and I explored the beautiful ranch on the gator often and fed Chico and Whisky (the horses) cookies every night. I planted flowers around the ranch and arena for her as a thank you for allowing us the time and space to breathe. I don't know what I would have done without Carol Ward. She was an angel sent from the Lord. I will forever be grateful to her.

We stayed at the ranch until August. School was starting, and I enrolled Brock in a Pre-K program. I found an affordable private school and got him settled, then after just two weeks, they called to tell me he was not ready for school. He had trigger traumas, and the staff was not equipped to deal with them. He had gaps in his emotional development that required time to heal. I was devastated. The only thing left for me to do was hire a nanny like I did during the summer to come sit with him while I worked.

I knew Carol would need her guest house back by September because of the NCHA Futurity. I didn't want to leave the ranch because it was my security. I felt safe there. The ranch hand, Fernando, was so sweet and made sure all of our needs were met. He even took Brock to get hay for the cows. Watching Brock become a secure little boy gave me hope. Still, I knew I had to find a place for us to live. My divorce was not final, so I couldn't purchase a home yet. The only thing I could do was find a home to lease until God made a way for us. On top of my legal and housing concerns, I owed the IRS $80,000.

Late fees continued to roll into the amount I owed, and I felt like I was drowning in debt.

The heaviness showed on me. I felt like I couldn't breathe. All I could do is keep working and hope I would land a large deal so I could get ahead. Financial stress is crippling and oppressive. I was determined I would get to a place where I would not depend on the next deal in order to provide for my family. This season taught me to allow the Lord to be my husband, to trust Him in all things, even when my pain feels deep and perpetual. Sometimes, I just get tired. But I do have a wonderful husband, and His name is the Great I Am.

Chapter 13

THE RIVER OF LIFE

I WAS SO GRATEFUL FOR OUR TIME OF REPRIEVE AT THE RANCH. Knowing I could not purchase until I got some things resolved, I set out to find something that felt permanent, but could be temporary. Naturally as a realtor, I had access to the latest properties that hit the market. I searched and searched. I loved the area where we lived. People were friendly, and the school system had been great for my little man. I drove through neighborhoods and looked at homes that I could lease within my budget, but nothing excited me. I looked at some new townhomes that had just been built, still nothing felt like home.

One day, Brock and I went to the local beach in the small town near us, and as he played in the sand, just loving life, I watched him and prayed to the Lord. I told Him we would live anywhere He provided. I told Him it would be so awesome if He would find us a place that we would love. It was a heartfelt prayer as a woman and a grandmother looking to create a warm home for herself and her grandson. It was not a childish demand.

On our drive back from the community beach on the lake, I was prompted to turn back into the neighborhood we had just left. I drove by a little home that we had looked at previously, and I told the Lord,

"This will be fine, and I am sorry I'm being so picky about where I will live." I felt like maybe I didn't appreciate what He brought. Suddenly something caught my eye! As I turned right to drive along the river, there was a brand new sign on a river home that was going live on the market the next day. I spoke to the agent on my phone as I sat in front of the house. The outside didn't look that appealing to me, but the agent described the inside, and I wanted to see it. Just then, the owner and the previous tenant walked out, so I asked the agent if I could see it now since someone was here.

I did! I walked into the door with the owners and fell absolutely in LOVE with this home. It was my favorite of all the homes I had lived in because it was right on the Brazos River, and the back of the home was all windows. It offered a totally remodeled kitchen, and it just *felt* like home. I can't explain the feeling, but to me, it was like Papa God was saying to me, "Baby Girl, I have you, and I will give you the desires of your heart. I know how you like to make a home, and I want you to be happy." It was a kiss from God. The simple gestures He does for me keep me going because I know He provides.

We settled into our new home. It was an absolute gift from God. Directly across the river is a beautiful horse ranch. My view is water and horses. God knew I loved water and horses. I began to feel like His favorite girl again. The house I had with my husband finally sold and our divorce was final November 1. I was excited to start a new year and make new memories.

The river house became my refuge. Brock and I moved in August of 2019. We love the summers as well as the winters. The neighborhood is full of children, and we live on the water. Our backyard is literally the Brazos. There's something about a river… a river flows and never gets stagnant. Its constant movement demonstrates to me how God always moves and flows through my life. He is never stagnate.

Brock and I settled in, and I made it the most warm and beautiful home. Brock is now five and doing so well. His mother is also doing great. She got help and is rebuilding her life. She is able to get Brock on weekends which blesses me too, so I can have some 'me' time.

Learning how to be a mom, Kiki, real estate agent, leader in the office, and have a social life takes mastery. I study things and read blogs to educate myself on today's toddlers. My goodness, this child gives me a run for my money. He is precious and I adore him, but it is hard because my Kiki role gets tangled up with my mommy role. I know the Lord has graced me during this season. I can't feel sorry for myself when my friends go on trips and do things I can't. I have to remember that God is faithful in this season. God also teaches me a lot about being a child. Brock has many triggers that I am getting help to understand how to deal with. I want to develop a leader and a strong young man. He is thriving in so many areas. He loves horses, so I want to find three retired cutting horses and purchase a small ranch in Weatherford and name it "Kiki Ranch." That is my dream. Brock loves the outdoors, and he is all boy.

My mom's health began failing. The horrible COVID pandemic hit and life as we know it shut down. I had never experienced such a season. My business went to nothing, the world seemed to be stopping right in front of my eyes. I am so grateful for my boy's grandfather and my sister who helped me get through a couple of months when cash flow was tough.

Because of COVID, I moved my office home to save money. I had to rethink how I did life, living and working from a small home and balance the workspace without sacrificing the feeling of home. I have an amazing view, and I love my haven on the river. I decided to move my mom to my home and care for her. It had reached a point that I couldn't go and see her often, and I was able to do this. My home only has two bedrooms, so I moved mom into Brock's room and put Brock with me. It was an adjustment, however caring for my mom was the best thing I could have done.

Mom and I made such good memories and she ate well. I enjoyed cooking for her, and it put me back in a role to nurture again. It was very nice. Watching my mom laugh during our movie nights was so soothing to my heart. She always had to have dessert with dinner. I think I even gained a few pounds during this season. It was such a blessing to have her with me.

Late September of 2020, Mom's oxygen levels dropped in the middle of night, and I had to call 9-1-1. She had to go to the hospital, where she stayed overnight. She never got strong after that visit. We had two other 9-1-1 scares, and it was during the last one that my mom died. I held her hand in the hospital room as she crossed over. That moment hit me with such gravity. I was alone with her and just could not leave the hospital room after she passed. I sat and cried for a good hour. The nurses kept coming to check on me. I just needed that breakdown because I don't think I had fully exhaled since December 19, 2018.

My family prepared for Mom's service, and it was beautiful. At the time of this writing, she has only been gone a number of months, and I still hear her voice. I miss her so much. I wasn't ready for her to go.

Naked and Unashamed is my life. I feel that perhaps my life is just now beginning. I am single, and I am raising my grandson, who is doing so well. I am profoundly grateful for him. This experience with him isn't what I planned, but I asked God to walk with me, and He was faithful. In February, a deal I had been working on for a couple of years came together, and with all of my closings for that month, I cleared over $110,000. I was able to pay everyone I owed money to. The previous year of my life, I found myself borrowing from everyone to make ends meet. But in February, I paid every person and a portion of my IRS bill and finally had a small amount in savings. God has been so good to me.

I don't know where my life will lead from here, but I do know that I love to broadcast hope to others because I know and understand difficult seasons firsthand. I feel like I have mastered walking through HELL and coming out the other side without the smell of smoke. Did I do it perfectly? No, I made a lot of mistakes in anger and the insecurities of abandonment, but I did the best I could.

I learned that I can survive every season of life, and I am still learning. Shame can paralyze a person. We have to just keep moving, pray always, and stay close to God. Walk in love, forgive freely, and keep moving forward. Allow God to guide you, and create the time you need in order to stay close to Him.

I worship my way through feeling alone and forgotten. I remember all the things He has saved me from. My life could have turned out so differently. Not that it is perfect now, but now I have peace. I know that God loves me and will guide me into the next chapter of my life. Nothing in my life has been easy. I have never had a princess life. Or maybe I do, and it just looks different than I imagined. I honestly think sometimes, *Father would you please just make this season a little easier for me? Let me breathe.*

I want to love again, but how can I even expect another person to take on what I have? I get it. It is a lot. But I know God is with me, and I don't have to worry. He has a plan for my life, and it is a plan to prosper me and not harm me. I trust that all I have gone through will help someone else. If my story inspires one person, it is worth getting naked and exposing the hardships of my life. It is worth being vulnerable to allow my scars to be visible. I made plenty of mistakes along the way, and I own those. He forgave me. I am His daughter, and I have no doubt God loves me. I claim to be His favorite, but the truth is we are all His favorite. He died for us all so that we can have life. Nothing is too big for Him, and He is never shocked at the things we do. He just wants our whole heart, and He requires us to hold Him up as our first love. Don't allow other things to take precedence over Him. I have done that, and it never ends well.

When all your pieces fall to the ground, pick them up one piece at a time and find yourself again. As soon as you begin making progress, there will be another season of challenge, and you will be a little more resilient and tenacious for the battle. I have learned in my life that triggers, bad experiences, abandonment, abuse, unresolved conflict, and withholding forgiveness can have tremendous power over your life. I am learning to trust God a little more than I ever have and to stay grateful in whatever season I am in. He is always faithful.

From childhood, I have fought for identity and belonging. I look at some of the choices I made and understand now why I fell into a lifestyle of drugs and every other predicament I landed in. My girlfriend Valarie always told me, "You will make it, you always do." My mom, Valarie, and Tammy always believed in me. It is funny, Tammy and my Mom are dancing with Jesus now. Valarie and I still see each other and talk often, even though she lives in another state. I cherish lifelong friendships.

I pray my story gives you hope. Our God is no respecter of persons. What I asked Him to do, He is doing for me even better than I imagined. His ways are so much better than mine, so much higher. Live life in curiosity. Live life believing the best for yourself. *One thing I finally really believed is that HE does LOVE me.* I believe that! I also believe He has an amazing plan for my life. When we look at situations through that lens, we embrace growth. If we are growing and living our best life possible, God always makes things better. He changes you before He changes situations.

God bless you in all you do. I pray we meet someday so I can hug you. You are uniquely made. Embrace YOU.

KIMBERLY OLIVER

CPSIA information can be obtained
at www.ICGtesting.com
Printed in the USA
LVHW070012090322
712906LV00010B/632